Careers for You Series

CAREERS FOR

CRAFTY PEOPLE

& Other Dexterous Types

MARK ROWH

THIRD EDITION

McGraw·Hill

New York   Chicago   San Francisco   Lisbon   London   Madrid   Mexico City
Milan   New Delhi   San Juan   Seoul   Singapore   Sydney   Toronto

The *McGraw·Hill* Companies

Library of Congress Cataloging-in-Publication Data

Rowh, Mark.
  Careers for crafty people & other dexterous types / by Mark Rowh. — 3rd ed.
      p.   cm. — (McGraw-Hill careers for you series)
      ISBN 0-07-145878-6 (alk. paper)
      1. Handicraft—Vocational guidance—United States.   I. Title.
  TT149.R68 2006
  745.5′023′73—dc22   2005021772

1 2 3 4 5 6 7 8 9 0   DOC/DOC   0 9 8 7 6

ISBN 0-07-145878-6

McGraw-Hill books are available at special quantity discounts to use as premiums and sales promotions, or for use in corporate training programs. For more information, please write to the Director of Special Sales, Professional Publishing, McGraw-Hill, Two Penn Plaza, New York, NY 10121-2298. Or contact your local bookstore.

This book is printed on acid-free paper.

CAREERS FOR

CRAFTY
PEOPLE

& Other Dexterous Types

. . . .

This book is dedicated to my friends
at New River Community College and
to all those crafty people who make
the world a more interesting place.

Contents

Foreword

nterested in a crafts-related career? If so, prepare for a truly challenging occupation. This career area, while requiring both creativity and patience, offers the potential to provide great job satisfaction.

Having a successful crafts career is like being a "plate spinner." You have to keep a lot of plates in midair at the same time to earn enough money to support yourself. It takes tenacity and a willingness to put in many hours to build a clientele and reputation that will enable you to support yourself through this work.

It's also important to bring your life's experience into whatever you do. I am an attorney, but my main occupation today is working as a designer and author on craft-related topics. While I rarely practice law anymore, I use my legal knowledge of intellectual property on an almost daily basis. Whatever your past education or work experience, be sure to apply it to your craft-related pursuits.

The most successful people in virtually any industry are rarely the most talented. There are a lot of very talented singers who never sing outside their own showers because they aren't willing to do what it takes to get their work seen and heard. If you are waiting for someone to discover you, you will have a long wait. The most successful artists in the craft industry are the people who get their work seen by the magazine editors; keep their face and name in front of the industry by attending seminars, conventions, and other industry events; and ask for work.

It isn't rocket science. Success requires tenacity and a passion for accomplishing your goals that is so strong that you can't even imagine it not happening for you. If you can put yourself in that frame of mind, then anything is possible!

Tera Leigh
Craft Author/Designer
Carlsbad, California
www.teraleigh.com

Acknowledgments

The author greatly appreciates the cooperation of the following individuals and organizations in the development of this book:

Henry Aitchison
American Association of Woodturners
American Bladesmith Society
American Craft Council
American Farriers Association
American Federation of Violin and Bow Makers
American Horticultural Therapy Association
American Institute of Organbuilders
American Watch Association
Arrowmont School of Arts and Crafts
Artist-Blacksmith Association of North America
Association of Medical Illustrators
Berea College
Blenko Glass Company
Book Manufacturers Institute
Doll Artisan Guild
Deb Erskine
Gemological Institute of America
Rachel Goldberger
Graphic Artists Guild
Greeting Card Association
Handweavers Guild of America

Haystack Mountain School of Crafts
Kathy Hudson
International Federation of Leather Guilds
International Guild of Candle Artisans
International Guild of Taxidermy
Kendall College of Art and Design
Knifemakers Guild
Landing School
National Association of Watch and Clock Collectors
National Council on Education for the Ceramic Arts
North Bennet Street School
Penna Omega
Peters Valley Craft Center
Kathy Peterson
Pilchuck Glass School
Professional Picture Framers Association
Rhode Island School of Design
Roberto-Venn School of Luthiery
Deborah Robson
Linda Rowh
Chris Saunders
Arthur Scharff
Society of American Florists
Society of North American Goldsmiths
Lisa Summerour
Texarkana College
Touchstone Center for Crafts
Violin Society of America
Virginia Mountain Crafts Guild

Introduction

E ven though we live in a world dominated by advanced technology, there is still a place for traditional handmade work. Have you ever admired a beautiful, old-fashioned quilt? Sipped tea from a handcrafted mug? Gazed upon a delicate, blown-glass vase? If so, you have appreciated the work of individual craftspeople.

Instead of churning out thousands of products in an assembly-line process, craftspeople tend to create their works one at a time, often by hand. They carry on an old tradition from our cultural past, producing items that show the stamp of individuality. Because their work differs so much from other occupations, many craftspeople pursue unusual careers and lifestyles. The work of a blacksmith or weaver, for example, is far removed from the office, the boardroom, or the typical factory. And that's the thrust of this book.

Careers for Crafty People & Other Dexterous Types profiles a wide range of careers in various craft areas. For some people, such careers fall too far outside the mainstream to be considered. But for others, such career possibilities represent a godsend—a chance to do work that is creative, different, and enjoyable. This book is directed to the latter group, as well as to those who may be in a position to influence potential craftspeople. I hope that the information presented here will be not only interesting but genuinely helpful to those making career plans that may include crafts.

CHAPTER ONE

Careers for Crafty People

There is a place in this world for crafty people. Are you one of them? *Crafty* here refers not to being clever or devious, but rather to having an eye for beauty. A crafty person is someone who takes basic materials such as wood, leather, metal, or glass and painstakingly transforms them into functional or decorative products. A crafty person uses patience and vision to create objects that are attractive, practical, or both. Usually, this means working with one's hands—as indicated by the "dexterous types" in this book's title. Also, crafty people take an individualized rather than an assembly-line approach to their work.

Being a crafty person can mean enjoying crafts as a hobby or even just reading and thinking about the possibilities in this area. But it can also form the foundation of an enjoyable and productive career. In an era of computers, fax machines, and space travel, there is still a place for people with the dedication to make things by hand and, in so doing, to enhance the lives of others with their creativity.

Crafty Success Stories

If you visit a crafts fair or simply check out artisan websites, you'll encounter people who have made a success of their interests in crafts. For some this has become a full-time career, while for others it is a part-time vocation.

For Rachel Goldberger of San Diego, California, an interest in crafts grew until she founded her own online baby boutique, Pink Confection. Rachel creatively repackages average baby bibs, hats, socks, and other items to create avant-garde gifts for expectant mothers. Her collections have been featured in publications such as *Self*, *Child*, *ePregnancy*, the *Washington Post*, and *Baby Talk* magazine.

Lisa Summerour of Columbus, Ohio, has taken an interest in family photographs and the scrapbooking industry as the impetus for a home-based business. She helps clients create legacy or heritage albums from the important photos and events in their lives. She enjoys the variety of working with traditional layouts that require few enhancements and coming up with creative designs using decorative paper and stickers.

Colorado-based Deborah Robson is a book and magazine editor specializing in craft-related subjects. She initially worked with silk screen on fabric and with weaving, selling her work through boutique shops, galleries, and fairs. She then turned to craft publishing and has edited magazines on spinning, weaving, and other topics while also working as a book and magazine author herself. She still works with fiber but spends more time doing writing, editing, layout, and design.

To Penna Omega of Los Angeles, a craft career means operating a small stationery and gifts business where she provides customized illustrations. She creates cartoons, caricatures, and other illustrations that can be printed on virtually anything. Recently, her works were featured in gift bags provided to celebrities appearing on the Grammy Awards show.

When Arthur Scharff of Seattle searched for a journal to write in, he was unhappy with the quality of books available in the general market. He decided to make his own leather journals and now offers leather "lifestyle" journals focusing on subjects ranging from wine making to hunting and fishing.

Your Own Success Story

Maybe you are a crafty person. If you're active now in one or more crafts—or if you have potential in such an area—then a crafts-related career may be a real possibility.

In considering such an option, it is important to realize that people such as those mentioned here do enjoy success at crafts-related careers. Certainly, careers in crafts fields are a far cry from the typical office or business setting, and sometimes following a crafts career can be risky, but others have made a go of it. Maybe you can, too! After all, there are a variety of job possibilities for crafty people.

Careers in Industry

Thousands of men and women hold industry jobs that involve the creation of objects of beauty. The glass industry is one example. Men and women in this industry make everything from dinnerware to ornamental vases. Another example is the jewelry industry. Someone makes all those gorgeous rings that make brides gasp. These workers are definitely crafty people! Ditto for those who create all kinds of products ranging from handmade leather belts to finely crafted wood products.

Of course, some jobs in industry revolve more around the operation of machinery for mass production than the individualized work most people would consider crafts. But within the overall manufacturing field, plenty of opportunities can be found for the creative and dexterous person.

Careers as Self-Employed Craftspeople

Probably the ultimate job for the crafty person is to function as a self-employed artisan. Here, the skills of a given craft form the basis for a small business. The concept is simple: you work at home (or in your own shop or studio), applying your creative talents to the production of items that appeal not only to yourself but also to customers who will pay enough money for your creations to keep you in business.

Sound far-fetched? Or too simplistic? The truth is, more than a hundred thousand people in the United States are currently self-employed as artists or craftspeople, according to the U.S. Department of Labor. This includes painters and sculptors as well as craft artists and printmakers. It does not include many thousands more who are self-employed in related areas ranging from photography to interior design.

Certainly, making a financial success of a self-run crafts business represents a challenge. But it can be done, as ambitious people throughout the United States and Canada have proved. Careers as self-employed craftspeople offer the promise of interesting work, creative freedom, and a chance to perform work that is far removed from that routinely done in offices and factories every day.

Careers in Education

Most craft areas are somewhat specialized. This means that newcomers need help in learning the techniques involved, and even those with experience can often benefit from additional instruction. Accordingly, there is a great demand for people who can teach various crafts to others.

Craft schools, community colleges, universities, art colonies, summer camps for children—these and other organizations employ people to teach in craft areas. Some schools specialize in one or two types of crafts. Others offer a wide range of subjects. The teachers they hire may be full-time educators or experienced craftspeople who teach part-time as a way to sharpen their own skills and enhance their incomes.

In any case, teaching offers an alternative career track for those interested in crafts. For those with the right skills and knowledge—and the ability to communicate with others—teaching can help make dreams of a crafts career a reality.

Careers Related to Crafts

Job possibilities also exist in areas that support the development and merchandising of crafts. Selling craft supplies, managing professional associations of people interested in crafts, and writing about crafts are several options. These occupations provide alternatives for those whose interests or skills do not include the creative process of the craft itself but who are interested in crafts.

Jobs in peripheral areas also provide working artisans with other career possibilities if they tire of making a living exclusively as craftspeople. In a related career, they can still be connected to the crafts world.

Advantages of a Crafts Career

A crafts career offers many advantages. First of all, it gives creative people a way to follow their true interests. One of the saddest situations in everyday life is the trapped feeling many people have about jobs they hold but do not like. Those with artistic abilities who follow crafts careers usually avoid this feeling. Instead, they work at something they actually enjoy doing!

Another advantage is that both part-time and full-time career paths can be followed. People who already have good jobs need not give them up. Homemakers, students, retired people, and others can decide just how much time they would like to devote to a craft-related endeavor, then proceed according to their own wishes. On the other hand, those who develop a broad enough base of financial support may make working as a craftsperson a full-time vocation.

Working at home is another plus. In many craft areas, most or all of the work can be performed at home. This is a real advantage for people who find it inconvenient to commute to and from the workplace on a daily basis. For example, parents of small children who prefer to provide their own child care instead of relying on baby-sitters or day care centers may find working at home advantageous. Similarly, people with physical disabilities can thrive in home-based craft businesses. For many disabled people, the home is the one place they find least challenging in terms of physical barriers.

In addition to these advantages, here are ten more reasons that a crafts career can be worth pursuing.

Ten Reasons to Consider a Crafts-Related Career

1. It can be fun.
2. You get to express yourself.
3. The end result is a tangible product featuring beauty, practicality, or both.
4. You don't have to dress up to do your daily work.
5. Many crafts careers provide the opportunity to operate your own business.
6. You don't need four years of college to prepare for many crafts careers.
7. The potential exists to earn a good income.
8. Selling the crafts you produce can provide a chance to socialize with customers and with other craftspeople.
9. If you are self-employed, you can set your own work schedule.
10. Making crafts can be less stressful than many other types of work, if it's something you truly enjoy.

Disadvantages of a Crafts Career

No career is absolutely perfect or devoid of risks. Like other career areas, work in a crafts field has its downside. A factor to keep in mind is that many craft areas depend on customers who have plenty of discretionary income; thus, craftspeople are particularly vulnerable to economic troubles. In a recession, an engraver is more likely to be out of work than is a nurse.

Not only are most craft areas highly dependent on economic conditions, but they require a large enough population to support sufficient business volume. This may make life difficult for craftspeople in sparsely populated areas, even though many crafts are associated with America's rural heritage. Quite often, it means that craftspeople must be willing to travel to arts and crafts fairs and exhibitions and to find other outlets for their work, such as wholesalers and distributors.

If your aim is to become wealthy, then this field may be a poor choice. While many artisans are able to support themselves through their work, few find that crafts lead them to affluence. But if wealth is less important to you than job satisfaction and other advantages, the financial rewards may still be satisfactory.

Do You Have the Right Qualifications?

A crafts career can be rewarding, but it won't be the right choice for everyone. Before pursuing work in this area, ask yourself the following questions:

1. Do you enjoy making things with your hands?
2. Do you have a good eye for details (such as shapes and colors)?
3. Are you patient? Can you work for a long period of time at a single task or series of tasks?
4. Are you creative?
5. Can you work well by yourself?
6. Are you a task-oriented person? Do you find satisfaction in completing one task and then going on to another?
7. Are you willing to go to school or to work under the supervision of someone else to learn special techniques?

8. Would you be willing to work in a shop-type environment?
9. Do you have the physical endurance to work at a craft for sufficient hours to be productive?
10. Can you maintain enough interest in a craft to make it more than just a hobby?

A Crafty Lifestyle

All things considered, one of the most attractive features of a crafts-related career is the alternative lifestyle it can make possible. This varies not only with the type of craft, but also with the specific job being done. Making jewelry, for instance, can be a highly standardized industrial process, where employees punch time clocks and work in an assembly-line mode. On the other hand, it can be a home-based business where the craftsperson sets his or her own working hours and exercises close control of the entire creative and production process.

It is the latter picture that fits more closely the role of the truly independent craftsperson. Doing what you want and controlling your own schedule may be just a dream for most people. But for those whose occupations consist of creating handcrafted items, a great deal of freedom is possible.

One craftsperson puts it this way: "It can be two o'clock on a hot Monday afternoon, and if I want to, I can be floating on an inner tube in the middle of the pond near my home. Sometimes it feels great to be doing something like that. I just close my eyes and picture all those people running around in three-piece suits and fighting the rat race."

Of course, that craftsperson may be working away late at night or on a weekend. But the trade-off is a sense of freedom that few careers can duplicate.

Career Options

Given the advantages of a crafts career, the next question might be: what types of jobs are available? The following chapters provide an overview of some of these career possibilities. If you are a crafty person—or you know someone who is—this book describes craft areas that anyone interested in this diverse occupational area might consider.

CHAPTER TWO

Into the Wood

Who doesn't like wood? It's among the most common of building materials, and it's one of the oldest. People have been working with wood since the dawn of history. For those with a crafty bent, it has provided material to be carved, cut, shaped, polished, and otherwise rendered into objects offering not just practicality but also great beauty. Today, craftspeople create an incredible array of products from wood.

Advantages of Wood

From soft white pine to durable oak, wood provides an attractive medium for crafts-related endeavors. Here are just some of the advantages of working with this unique material:

- **Wood is plentiful.** Despite the concerns of some environmentalists, there is plenty of wood in the world. North America still has more trees than it needs, and current strategies of replacing trees with new ones will assure this in the future.
- **Wood is affordable.** Sure, a trip to the local lumber store can be an eye-opener. Costs seem especially high when compared with prices of a generation ago. But when compared with other materials, wood is still a reasonably priced commodity. Craftspeople can afford to purchase wood, add the cost of their labor, and still come up with products affordable to consumers.

- **Wood can be beautiful.** When handled with care and skill, wood provides an extremely beautiful construction material. Who can dispute the attractiveness of an elegant cherry table or mahogany chair?
- **Wood offers variety.** Because there are so many varieties and grades of wood, those who work with it can choose from a wide range of basic materials. Whatever the task at hand, some type of wood will most likely be able to meet the need.

The types of jobs that involve woodcraft are surprisingly diverse. The following overviews present some of the most interesting of these career options.

Furniture Maker

Making furniture is one of the most basic of craft areas. It is also one of the most promising from a business viewpoint, since the items produced are functional in nature and, therefore, appeal to a widely diverse audience.

An advantage with this craft area is that special training may not be necessary, nor are unusual artistic talents required. Certainly, it helps to have good manual skills, a flair for working with wood, and an eye for symmetry. But beyond these basic traits, virtually anyone can learn the fundamentals of making some type of furniture.

When it comes to furniture making, you can take the route of simplicity or of complex design and development. For example, one approach is to concentrate on just a few basic items. The first step is obtaining a design for one type of furniture, such as a stool or a bookshelf. This might be a drawing of one's own design or a copy of an existing piece of furniture. The craftsperson then simply duplicates as many copies of the original as time allows and market conditions will support.

Typical examples of furniture items that can be made in this manner include:

- full-sized rocking chairs
- children's rocking chairs
- chests
- toy boxes
- stools
- bookshelves
- porch swings
- toolboxes

As skills develop, the experienced furniture maker may choose to vary designs and emphasize individuality rather than replication of a few basic designs. Under this approach, the development of new and different pieces is an important component of the craft. At any rate, making handcrafted furniture can provide more than enough variety to keep an ambitious craftsperson busy and challenged.

Furniture Designer

Closely connected with making furniture is designing it as an artistic venture. Here, furniture is seen not just as a utilitarian item but also as a form of art.

Some people explore furniture design in special workshops, classes, or extended programs of study. Many schools and craft centers offer courses in designing and making furniture. An example is the Anderson Ranch Arts Center in Snowmass Village, Colorado, which offers workshops ranging from wood turning to designing and making writing desks.

It is even possible to earn a college degree in furniture design. Kendall College of Art and Design, a part of Ferris State University in Grand Rapids, Michigan, offers a bachelor's degree with a furniture design major. This is anything but a trendy new program, having been in existence since 1928, yet it is quite up-to-date, even including instruction in the latest computer design techniques. Students in this program learn to design wood furniture products that can be manufactured by the furniture industry; thus, their work centers more on the design of furniture than its actual production. In the process, though, students often build prototypes of their creations.

Typical courses in this program include the following:

- Introduction to Furniture Design
- Portfolio Development
- Drafting/Introduction to Detailing
- CAD Detailing
- Furniture Studio
- Ornaments
- Detailing I, II, III, and IV
- Furniture Design I and II
- Furniture Construction
- Furniture Design Thesis
- Furniture Design Portfolio

In addition to courses in the program, students take the basic subjects needed for a college degree, including English and other general studies courses.

A college degree in furniture design? Can't I just study existing furniture and then come up with my own variations? The answer is, of course you can! The Kendall College plan just represents one option. You can also enroll in a short course such as those offered by the Anderson Ranch Arts Center or the Center for Furniture Craftsmanship.

The Center for Furniture Craftsmanship is a year-round, non-profit woodworking school in Rockport, Maine, offering classes in furniture making, design, and related skills such as carving, turning, and finishing. Students include novice, intermediate, advanced, and professional woodworkers. A twelve-week intensive session is designed for those who are considering furniture making as a profession or as a part-time career or hobby. It consists of twelve consecutive weeks of hands-on woodworking with daily personal instruction. A nine-month curriculum is also available, as are one- and two-week workshops on specific topics related to furniture design. Students come from across the United States and around the world, and instructors are professional furniture makers and wood turners.

Another approach is to learn as much as you possibly can about furniture—read books on the subject, prowl around furniture stores and antique shops—and then try your hand at a few simple designs.

Once you master the basics of designing furniture, you may want to operate solely in this area. Or, like many craftspeople, you can combine the skills of furniture design with the actual practice of furniture making. For more information, contact:

Anderson Ranch Arts Center
PO Box 5598
5263 Owl Creek Road
Snowmass Village, CO 81615
www.andersonranch.org

Center for Furniture Craftsmanship
25 Mill Street
Rockport, ME 04856
www.woodschool.org

Kendall College of Art and Design of Ferris State University
17 Fountain Street
Grand Rapids, MI 49503
www.kcad.edu

Cabinetmaker

Cabinetmaking is a major occupation in the woodworking field. Obviously, this specialty is closely related to making furniture of other types. However, cabinetmakers tend to focus on a few basic items: cabinets, shelves, counters, and related structures used in homes and businesses for storage or work space.

Another distinguishing feature of this field is that work may be done not only in a shop or factory but also on-site in homes or businesses. In one instance, a cabinetmaker may build kitchen cabinets in a shop and then install them in a customer's home. In another case, the cabinetmaker might do the basic construction where it is to be located, installing a set of built-in shelves that are not designed to be portable.

In the spectrum of careers that involve working with wood, cabinetmaking would probably fall somewhere in the middle. The work generally is not as artistic as that of wood carving, nor is it as elemental and varied as carpentry, which may involve building anything from crude wooden forms for pouring concrete to the rough structures of inner walls and subfloors.

Cabinetmakers' work is careful, methodical, and precise. Their work is production oriented, but it also has its creative side. Choosing a cabinet design or creating a new one can be a challenging process. Similarly, putting just the right finish on a shelf or cabinet often requires an artistic touch.

Cabinetmakers use tools and techniques not greatly different from those of others who work with wood. They learn their craft in any of several ways, from classes or seminars to on-the-job training.

Perhaps the best way to get started in this field is to hire out to an experienced cabinetmaker and learn the craft as an employee. Studying books and magazine articles on the subject can also help (see the list at the end of this chapter).

Wood Turner

Wood turners produce beautiful work that is sometimes purely decorative. To do this fascinating craft, they use lathes or other equipment to cut, shape, and polish wood. The results range from original sculptures to unusual wood containers, as these examples demonstrate:

- A New York wood turner produces segmented turnings that resemble woven and stitched baskets.
- A Washington-based craftsperson makes turnings that emulate desert scenes and other landscapes.
- A Vermont wood turner makes attractive lidded containers.

Other wood turners produce large and small sculptures, holiday ornaments, goblets, various kinds of vessels, and other items.

While some men and women practice wood turning as a hobby, others pursue it as a part-time or full-time career. Many specialize in just a few types of products, while others take a more broad-based approach. They sell their work through galleries, crafts fairs, trade shows, and direct marketing.

The first step to becoming a wood turner, normally, is learning to use a lathe. Then it takes patience and practice to learn the craft. One way to get started in wood turning is to enroll in a course or seminar on the subject at a local community college or adult education program. Another way is to contact someone who works in this area and work out an apprenticeship or other plan for working with, and learning from, an experienced wood turner.

Anyone who is serious about wood turning as a career should take advantage of membership in the American Association of Woodturners (AAW). This group has more than eleven thousand members in more than 230 local chapters across the United States and is also open to members from Canada and other countries.

The AAW is the publisher of a quarterly journal, *American Woodturner*. A staple of this magazine is how-to information on various aspects of wood turning. It also includes valuable information on topics ranging from book reviews to safety tips.

An annual highlight is a three-day symposium held in a different part of the country each year. The event includes demonstrations by recognized wood turners, an "instant gallery" where members can display their work, and a trade show.

Of special note is the group's scholarship program, which provides funds to attend classes in wood turning offered by a number of craft schools. Only AAW members are eligible to receive scholarship funds. For more information:

American Association of Woodturners
222 Landmark Center
75 West Fifth Street
St. Paul, MN 55102
www.woodturner.org

Wood-Carver

Wood-carvers play a unique role in the world of arts and crafts. They produce decorative and artistic items, as well as make functional items more attractive.

Some craftspeople use power equipment—sometimes even a chain saw—to produce carvings. Others work entirely by hand, using chisels, knives, or other hand-cutting tools.

To make a go of working full-time at their craft, many wood-carvers specialize in a single type of product or a series of related items. Here are just some examples:

- carving fish, ducks, or other animals to cater to the interests of hunters and others with a love of the outdoors
- creating wooden busts or statues

- producing items related to local or regional culture (such as figures of mountaineers and other Appalachian characters in the southeastern United States)
- carving canes or walking sticks for use in hiking

In some instances, craftspeople in this field apply their skills to materials other than wood. For instance, animal bones may be used as an alternative to wood. The same is true of deer or elk antlers. And some enterprising carvers have learned to use a nut-based substitute for ivory as a raw material that meets today's standards for protecting endangered species.

Toy Maker

In the age of hand-held electronic games, is there still a place for wooden toys? Perhaps surprisingly, the answer is a very definite yes. Not only do today's computer-literate children still enjoy playing with wooden toys, but many adults will go out of their way to purchase "old-fashioned" toys for their children and grandchildren. There is something inherently satisfying about a genuine wood toy, especially one that has been handcrafted.

Craftspeople who make toys produce a wide variety of items, including dinosaurs, trains, carousel animals, and guns. Wooden toys are often popular items at craft shows. They are also sold to specialty shops and other retailers (for instance, toy wooden cannons might be sold to a store that features Civil War merchandise). For those who enjoy making them, wooden toys can be an adjunct to other types of woodworking or an area of special focus.

Guitar Maker

To be a successful craftsperson from a career viewpoint, one must create products that are in significant demand by the public at large or that meet the needs of a specific interest group. People who make guitars fit into the both categories. After all, guitars are among the most popular of instruments. The glamour of rock and roll, the popularity of country music, and the appeal of other types of music involving guitars mean that these instruments are in great demand. This is true not only for professional musicians, who often treasure handcrafted instruments, but also for countless music lovers who simply enjoy playing guitars.

People who make guitars may operate their own businesses or work for companies that manufacture and sell musical instruments. Some build only acoustic guitars; others specialize in electric guitars; still others make both kinds of instruments. Although other materials may be used, wood is still a basic building material. Favorite woods for this purpose include mahogany, spruce, cedar, and rosewood, with different types of wood used for different parts of the instrument.

The Roberto-Venn School of Luthiery in Phoenix, Arizona, provides a comprehensive program in guitar making and repair. The basic course consists of 880 hours of instruction offered over a four-month period. During this time, every student constructs at least one acoustic and one electric guitar or bass. For more information, contact the school:

Roberto-Venn School of Luthiery
4011 South Sixteenth Street
Phoenix, AZ 85040
www.roberto-venn.com

Violin Maker

Among the most specialized of all woodcrafts is the art of making violins. This work rests on centuries of tradition, including master craftspeople such as Antonio Stradivari, whose seventeenth-century violins are considered perhaps the finest ever made.

Because violins play a central role in orchestras and other highly formal musical settings, they must be made to exacting standards. Violin makers work slowly and carefully, and their work may be subject to review by others in the field.

Unlike some craft areas, violin making is not something that can be readily self-taught. Perhaps the best way to get started is to contact a practicing violin maker and discuss possibilities for learning the craft as an apprentice.

The American Federation of Violin and Bow Makers publishes a directory of its members in the United States, Canada, and Britain. To contact a member, see the directory on the organization's website, write to the address at the end of this section, or check the yellow pages in your phone book to see if a craftsperson is listed.

The Violin Society of America, whose members include both those who make and those who play these instruments, is another source of information.

For more information, contact:

American Federation of Violin and Bow Makers
1201 South Main Street
Mount Airy, MD 21771
www.afvbm.com

The Guild of American Luthiers
8222 South Park Avenue
Tacoma, WA 98408
www.luth.org

Violin Society of America
48 Academy Street
Poughkeepsie, NY 12601
www.vsa.to

Traditional Instrument Maker

In the Old World and later in Colonial America, a variety of hand-made instruments were popular, including banjos, mandolins, dulcimers, and other related instruments. Some of these instruments are still made today.

The Appalachian dulcimer, for example, is a three- or four-string instrument made in either a teardrop or hourglass shape. Built of walnut or cherry, the beautiful instruments are popular with traditional musicians as well as those interested in music and culture of the past.

Another example is the hammer dulcimer. These larger instruments, constructed of maple and red cedar, are played with a small hammer not unlike that used for a xylophone.

The craftsperson who chooses to make traditional instruments can gain satisfaction not only from the work itself but also in the knowledge that the culture of the past is being preserved. To learn more about this unique craft area, visit a crafts fair or a performance by musicians using traditional instruments and talk with those involved. Some summer arts and crafts programs also offer classes or seminars on making traditional instruments.

Boat Builder

Another specialized field within woodworking is boat building. People who construct wooden boats fill a unique niche. They build various types of boats, with sailboats as perhaps the most glamorous.

Workers in this field may specialize in constructing small boats, building cruising boats, or designing various types of craft. They may be employed by companies that build boats and ships, by design firms, or by marine supply companies. Others operate their own businesses building or repairing boats.

A school that specializes in this field offers students complete ten-month programs in either boat building or design. For more information:

Landing School
PO Box 1490
Kennebunkport, ME 04046
www.landingschool.org

Other Woodcraft Jobs

Many more specialties exist in the woodworking field. Here are a few more brief examples:

- **Model maker.** Some people specialize in building wooden models of boats, buildings, or other structures. For example, one artisan builds small wooden replicas of airplanes. Pilots and other flight lovers buy the small pieces not as toys but as decorations or mementos.
- **Birdhouse maker.** Birdhouses are popular items everywhere. Some craftspeople build birdhouses and feeders and then sell them in various versions: painted, unpainted, fully assembled, or partially assembled.
- **Mantel maker.** In older homes, mantels above fireplaces were a staple. A South Carolina craftsperson has found there is a growing demand for mantels in newer homes as well. He operates a full-time business designing, building, and installing mantels of various sizes and configurations.
- **Carpenter.** Carpenters represent a more mainstream craft than many others discussed in this chapter, but they apply similar skills, use the same kinds of tools, and offer the chance for interesting, gratifying work. From building a storage shed or constructing temporary scaffolding to

installing finely crafted molding in a home or office, carpenters perform a wide range of tasks.

- **Preservation carpenter.** Workers in this more specialized field of carpentry help restore and preserve historic buildings and other items. They use traditional techniques to create authentic-looking results.
- **Wood burner.** Instead of carving, practitioners of this craft burn images into wood. The letters and graphic designs that result combine both practical and decorative features. For example, some works serve as simple signs, while others represent artistic creations.
- **Furniture restorer.** This field involves refinishing and otherwise restoring older furniture. Some furniture restorers handle only the finishes of furniture, while others reconstruct portions of damaged pieces by utilizing skills similar to those required for making furniture.

Further Reading

Books

Bennett, David, and Roger Schroeder. *Step-by-Step Relief Carving: Mastering the Use of Light and Perspective in Woodcarving.* Fox Chapel Publishing Company, 2003.

Blackburn, Graham. *Traditional Woodworking Handtools: An Illustrated Reference Guide for the Woodworker.* Lyons Press, 1999.

Bridgewater, Gill, and Alan Bridgewater. *Woodcarving Basics.* Sterling Publishing Company, 2002.

English, Jim. *Making a Laminated Hollowbody Electric Guitar.* Authorhouse, 2005.

Hillyer, John. *Woodcarving: 20 Great Projects for Beginners and Weekend Carvers.* Lark Books, 2002.

Hunnex, John. *Woodturning Forms and Materials.* Guild of Master Craftsman Publications, 2004.

Kinkead, Jonathan. *Build Your Own Acoustic Guitar*. Hal Leonard Corporation, 2004.

Middleton, Rik. *Guitar Maker's Workshop*. Crowood Press, 2004.

Nish, Dale. *Woodturning with Ray Allen: A Master's Designs & Techniques for Segmented Bowls & Vessels*. Fox Chapel Publishing, 2004.

Norbury, Ian. *Carving Classic Female Figures in Wood: A How-to Reference for Carvers and Sculptors*. Fox Chapel Publishing, 2004.

Olsen, Tim, and Cyndy Burton (Editors). *Lutherie Woods and Steel String Guitars: A Guide to Tonewoods with a Compilation of Repair and Construction Techniques*. Guild of American Luthiers, 1998.

Peters, Rick. *Popular Mechanics Workshop: Scroll Saw Fundamentals: The Complete Guide*. Hearst Books, 2005.

Rae, Andy. *The Complete Illustrated Guide to Furniture and Cabinet Construction*. Taunton Press, 2001.

Raffan, Richard. *Taunton's Complete Illustrated Guide to Turning*. Taunton Press, 2005.

Raffan, Richard. *Turning Wood with Richard Raffan*. Taunton Press, 2001.

Self, Charlie. *Woodworker's Pocket Reference: Everything a Woodworker Needs to Know at a Glance*. Fox Chapel Publishing, 2005.

Siminoff, Roger. *The Luthier's Handbook: A Guide to Building Great Tone in Acoustic Stringed Instruments*. Hal Leonard Corporation, 2001.

Tibbetts, Malcolm. *The Art of Segmented Wood Turning: A Step-by-Step Guide*. Linden Publishing, 2004.

Walters, Sue. *Pyrography Workbook: A Complete Guide to Woodburning*. Fox Chapel Publishing, 2005.

Williams, Jack A., and Rick Jensen. *Illustrated Guide to Carving Tree Bark: Releasing Whimsical Houses and Woodspirits from Found Wood*. Fox Chapel Publishing, 2004.

Magazines

American Woodworker
Home Service Publications
260 Madison Avenue
New York, NY 10016
www.rd.com/americanwoodworker

Carving Magazine
PO Box 500
Mt. Morris, IL 61054
www.carvingmagazine.com

Fine Woodworking
63 South Main Street
PO Box 5507
Newtown, CT 06470
www.finewoodworking.com

Woodsmith
PO Box 842
Des Moines, IA 50304
www.woodsmith.com

Woodworker's Journal
PO Box 56585
Boulder, CO 80322
www.woodworkersjournal.com

CHAPTER THREE

All That Glitters

The human eye has always been attracted to beauty—especially the kind that shines or glitters. From the tombs of the pharaohs to the palaces of eighteenth-century Europe and into the present, people from all types of cultures and all walks of life have placed special value on items that catch light and reflect or refract it. If the materials from which such objects were made held great value, such as precious jewels or metals, so much the better.

People who can work with jewels or various kinds of metal have long been in demand. Today, craftspeople in a wide range of specialty areas meet the needs for finely crafted objects made of these materials.

Jewelry Maker

Want to work at a craft that is not only creative but also a great source of potential profits? If so, consider the role of jewelry maker. This craft combines the pleasure of creating beautiful work with the practicality of a product for which people will pay a premium. While some products appeal only to customers with specialized interests (for example, dulcimers or mandolins), jewelry holds value to almost anyone. Even those who are not in the market for jewelry for themselves may be potential buyers of gift items for relatives and friends.

Jewelry makers may be known by any of several titles, including jeweler, jewelry jobber, and jewelry repairer. They design, construct, and repair all types of jewelry, including rings, necklaces, bracelets, pins, and earrings. Their work is not only artistic but also very detailed and quite precise.

Some workers who make jewelry operate in a manufacturing setting. A typical job might involve placing gems in rings as part of a team assembling jewelry in a factory.

Another job might consist of cleaning and repairing jewelry as a staff member in a jewelry store. Other jobs, including those pursued by many craftspeople, involve designing and making pieces as a small business.

Jewelers usually develop their skills through on-the-job training or by attending a trade or technical school. Those who attend trade schools take classes in such subjects as basic jewelry making skills, repair techniques, and use of tools and machines. Programs normally take two years or less to complete.

Gem Cutter

A less common occupation than jewelry maker—but a very important related one—is that of gem cutter. Gem cutters take rough gemstones and cut, grind, or polish them into the gleaming gems needed to make beautiful rings, necklaces, bracelets, and other types of jewelry.

Some gem cutters work for jewelry companies. Others operate their own businesses. In the latter case, they either work on a contractual basis for wholesale or retail firms, or they directly purchase uncut gems and then sell them after rendering them usable for jewelry.

Even more than in most craft areas, working as a gem cutter requires patience. In fact, it takes a very special type of personality to be able to succeed in, and to enjoy, this unique field. Successful gem cutters are able to sit quietly in one position for long periods of time. They have (or are able to develop) a knack for pacing themselves, working quickly enough to be productive, yet slowly and carefully enough to avoid costly mistakes. The latter is a key consideration. Mistakes in gem cutting can be disastrous, given the value that precious gems usually carry.

Not only is the work precise and painstaking, but it also involves a certain sense of vision. A gem cutter must be able to take a rough hunk of material and in his or her mind's eye see it as a lovely, shining gem. Then, the cutter must employ the necessary techniques to bring about such a transformation. This usually involves cutting or grinding the gem in such a way that any extraneous material is removed, and shaping (such as facets) is added to reflect light and enhance the stone's beauty. The mental effort involved might be compared to that of a champion chess player, who must envision moves far in advance of making them. In shaping the material at hand, the gem cutter must think ahead, anticipate problems, and make the most of each cut or change.

In addition to the demands of the work itself, gem cutting is a challenging vocation. This is especially true of the independent gem cutter. Such a role may require a substantial financial investment. Special tools, such as diamond saws, are necessary. In addition, the expense of purchasing gems such as rubies, sapphires, and emeralds—even in a rough state—can be significant.

To learn about gem cutting, a good starting point is to take a class on the subject. Classes in gem cutting are sometimes offered by community colleges or other schools. Even classes designed more for hobbyists than for professionals can prove helpful. Whatever the starting point, many elements of the craft can only be learned by actual practice in cutting gems. Working first with semiprecious stones or others of modest value is wise. Offering to work with an experienced gem cutter as an assistant or informal apprentice is another way to get started.

The Gemological Institute of America is a major school offering training in this area. Campuses are located in several cities around the world. For information on campuses in the United States, contact:

Gemological Institute of America
5345 Armada Drive
Carlsbad, CA 92008
www.gia.edu

....

Watchmaker

How about a career in horology? Horology—the art of making watches, or, more generally, the study of time—is an occupation that has flourished for several hundred years. Watchmakers have long enjoyed working at a craft that is highly specialized, always in demand, and financially rewarding.

The term *watchmaker* is generally used to refer not just to constructing watches but also repairing them. In fact, much of the need for workers in this field comes in the latter category.

Few people would challenge the notion that watchmaking is indeed a craft. Those who master this complex process do detailed, precise work that can include the creative process of watch or clock design as well as the more mechanical functions of watch maintenance and repair. The products with which watchmakers, like jewelry makers, deal are often regarded as much for their beauty as their functionality. Working with an expensive luxury watch, for instance, can be compared with building or repairing an intricate bracelet, ring, or necklace.

Despite some changes in watch technology, prospects for a career in watchmaking remain strong. Some people were predicting the demise of traditional watchmaking and repair due to the advent of digital watches and other electronic models, but the field has survived such changes and made something of a comeback. Mechanical watches remain popular, especially expensive brand-name varieties. As a result, consumers still have significant needs for the services of skilled watchmakers and repairers. In fact, the need for new workers in this field is expected to be quite strong in the next ten to fifteen years, as more and more working watchmakers reach retirement age.

To practice their craft, watchmakers and repairers must learn how different types of watches operate and then master the use of appropriate tools. These tools include special lathes, grinding wheels, and electronic testing and regulating equipment. Watchmakers also use various types of measurement equipment such as metric scales, balances, and micrometers; optical equipment such as microscopes; and ultrasound cleaning equipment. Their work is done at a workbench, and the surrounding environment is usually clean and relatively quiet as opposed to that of a machine shop or factory floor.

As with other craft areas, watchmakers enjoy the option of working for themselves or of seeking jobs in industry or in retail. Typical employers include watch factories, jewelry stores, department stores, and shops specializing in the repair of jewelry and watches.

For those who prefer to operate their own businesses, watchmaking offers unusual opportunities. Since there is not a surplus of trained watchmakers and repairers (but rather a shortage in many parts of the country), small businesses in this field may encounter fewer problems in generating business than in many other craft areas that may be considered less essential to the ordinary customer.

In order to start their own businesses, some watchmakers rent bench space, while others set up operations in a garage or portion of their homes. Some develop contracts with watch manufacturers or retail establishments that sell large numbers of watches. Others prefer to deal directly with individual customers.

The precise nature of watchmaking requires special training. This is available through a number of community colleges, technical colleges, and trade schools.

The National Association of Watch and Clock Collectors operates the NAWCC School of Horology, which is designed to continue the tradition of watch and clock repair. The school offers both clock repair and watch repair programs. Students study at the beginner, intermediate, and advanced levels.

Course offerings include:

- Horological Lathes
- Introduction to Watch Repair
- Staffing, Jewelling, and Escapements
- Hairsprings
- Wristwatches
- Battery Watches
- Making Parts
- Repair Problems
- Specialized Repairs
- Chime Clock Repair
- Introduction to Escapements
- Four Hundred Day & Cuckoo Clocks
- Antique Long Case Clocks
- Platform Escapements
- Machine Tools and Their Use in Clock Making

For more information, contact:

National Association of Watch and Clock Collectors
   (NAWCC)
School of Horology
514 Poplar Street
Columbia, PA 17512
www.nawcc.org

Because of the shortage of watchmakers in some areas, it may be possible to obtain financial sponsorship from an employer or prospective employer. In such cases, the employer may pay all or part of the student's tuition or other educational costs.

Watchmaking skills are readily transferable to other occupations. Thus, pursuing a career in watchmaking, especially trying to make a success of a one-person business, is not as risky as in some other craft areas. Experienced watchmakers and repairers can find jobs in other areas requiring a high skill level, such as instrumentation or electronics.

For more information, contact:

American Watch Association
1201 Pennsylvania Avenue NW
PO Box 464
Washington, DC 20044
www.watchmakereducation.com

American Watchmakers-Clockmakers Institute
701 Enterprise Drive
Harrison, OH 45030
www.awci.com

Canadian Clock Museum
60 James Street
Deep River, ON K0J 1P0
Canada
www.canclockmuseum.ca

Blacksmith

Blacksmiths, once an essential part of every village or town, still flourish, if in much smaller numbers than in our agrarian past. Many run their own one-person shops.

As in past times, working with horseshoes is a major source of business. Blacksmiths who shoe horses are also known as farriers.

Blacksmiths also construct collars, farm utensils, tools, and other practical items. Some make objects that are designed more for artistic purposes. Others specialize in a specific line of items, such as skillets or other kitchen utensils.

The skills needed by a blacksmith can be mastered on an individual basis while working for or studying under an experienced blacksmith. Another approach is to take classes or summer workshops. One place to learn such techniques is the Touchstone Center for Crafts in Farmington, Pennsylvania, where students enroll in workshops such as these:

- Beginning Blacksmithing
- Traditional Architectural Blacksmithing
- Advanced Metals
- Kitchen Smithing

For more information on the school, contact:

Touchstone Center for Crafts
1049 Wharton Furnace Road
Farmington, PA 15437
www.touchstonecrafts.com

Mesalands Community College

Another example of such a program is the Farrier Science program offered by Mesalands Community College, where students can become familiar with the basics of the farrier business while also developing the necessary skills to become a farrier. Students learn to work with anvils, forges, vises, and other specialty hand tools.

This program offers two options. The most basic is a sixteen-week certificate program involving nineteen credit hours of horse anatomy, business, blacksmithing, horseshoeing, and theory. The second option is a two-year associate's degree with an emphasis on farrier science. The degree offers a more in-depth, timely program. Typical skills acquired by students include:

- horsemanship
- cold shoeing
- hot shoeing

- blacksmithing
- therapeutic shoeing

The classroom portion of the program includes such courses as:

- Anatomy
- Physiology
- Horseshoeing Theory
- Business Management
- Lameness

For more information, contact:

Mesalands Community College
911 South Tenth Street
Tucumcari, NM 88401
www.mesalands.edu

Equine Education Institute

An interesting distance learning option is offered by Equine Education Institute. It is designed for those who would like to become farriers as well as those who would like to trim and shoe their own horses. The course is approved by the Illinois Department of Vocational Education and has been designated a Master Educator School by the Brotherhood of Working Farriers.

Students complete the following three modules using videotapes or DVDs and accompanying texts:

- Trimming the Foot, which covers trimming horses' feet, including anatomy, physiology, safety, tools, and balance
- Basic Shoeing, which includes selecting shoes, fitting shoes, nailing, and finishing
- Certification, which includes beginning forge techniques and skills, and prepares students for the certification

examinations offered by the American Farriers Association or the Brotherhood of Working Farriers (BWFA)

For more information, contact:

Equine Education Institute
PO Box 68
Ringwood, IL 60072
www.equus.com

For information on other programs, check out these schools:

College of Veterinary Medicine
Veterinary Medical Teaching Hospital
Cornell University
Ithaca, NY 14853
www.cornell.edu

Colorado School of Trades
1575 Hoyt Street
Lakewood, CO 80215
www.schooloftrades.com

Kentucky Horseshoeing School
Highway 53 South
PO Box 120
Mt. Eden, KY 40046
www.kyhorseshoeing.com

Kwantlen University College
12666 Seventy-Second Avenue
Surrey, BC V3W 2M8
Canada
www.kwantlen.ca

Montana State University
Department of Animal and Range Sciences
Horseshoeing School
PO Box 172900
Bozeman, MT 59717
www.animalrange.montana.edu

Pacific Coast Horseshoeing School
9625 Florin Road
Sacramento, CA 95829
www.farrierschool.com

Walla Walla Community College
Farrier Program
500 Tausick Way
Walla Walla, WA 99362
www.wwcc.edu

Wolverine Farrier School
3104 East Stevenson Lake Road
Clare, MI 48617
www.wfschool.com

For additional information about horseshoeing, contact:

American Farriers Association
4059 Iron Works Parkway, Suite 1
Lexington, KY 40511
www.americanfarriers.org

Another organization of interest is the Artist-Blacksmith Association of North America (ABANA). This group serves those interested in blacksmithing as an art form. The group sponsors conferences, exhibitions, publications, and other activities. It also maintains a library of slides, CDs, and videotapes showing works of blacksmiths from around the world. For information, contact:

Artist-Blacksmith Association of North America (ABANA)
PO Box 816
Farmington, GA 30638
www.abana.org

Goldsmith and Silversmith

Goldsmiths work with gold and other precious metals. They make a variety of ornamental items, including jewelry, desk accessories, medallions, and chains. While some goldsmiths work independently, many others work for jewelry firms or other companies.

Silversmiths do very similar work, but they use silver as their primary working material. They often produce tableware and related items in addition to jewelry and other ornamental work.

Persons interested in this craft area should consider joining the Society of North American Goldsmiths (SNAG), headquartered in Tampa, Florida. While the title of the organization refers only to gold, its members work in a variety of materials, including silver, copper, brass, nickel, and other metals, as well as nonmetallic substances such as polymer clays, marble, quartz, pearl, and coral.

Like organizations in other craft areas, SNAG provides members a forum for networking with others who share the same interests. Members can take advantage of an annual conference, exhibitions of fine metalwork, and publications of interest. These include *Metalsmith*, a quarterly magazine, as well as a bimonthly newsletter that includes information on exhibitions, conferences, and workshops. It also lists job opportunities in the field, an extremely helpful feature for anyone interested in pursuing employment as a goldsmith or silversmith. For more information, contact:

Society of North American Goldsmiths
1300 Iroquois Avenue, Suite 160
Naperville, IL 60563
www.snagmetalsmith.org

....

Knife Maker

Knife makers, or bladesmiths, use various techniques to construct knives. The most accomplished use forging methods to create knife blades from steel, nickel, or other metals. Bladesmiths also use techniques such as grinding, filing, and annealing. They make handles of different materials, including wood, plastic, or such traditional materials as bone.

Traditional bladesmiths do most of their work by hand. Some operate their own shops and businesses.

Those who are seriously interested in a knife making career might consider attending the Bill Moran School of Bladesmithing offered through Texarkana College of Texarkana, Texas, in cooperation with the American Bladesmith Society. This unique school offers intensive classes lasting one or two weeks each, making it possible for people from around the country to attend. Courses are taught by recognized bladesmiths from Texas, Arkansas, and all across the United States who teach through special arrangements with the school. Class sessions are held in Washington, Arkansas, in a replica of a one-room schoolhouse and adjacent barn. The facility includes a modern classroom as well as equipment such as forges, grinders, workbenches, and a trip-hammer. Students and faculty stay in a local hotel that offers special rates to those connected with the school.

Students may enroll in courses such as the following:

- **Introduction to Bladesmithing.** Taught over a two-week period, this course covers the hand forging of blades.

Through both lecture and hands-on work, students learn to select metal and make blades through hammer forging, annealing, heat treating, grinding, and tempering.

- **Handles and Guards.** Students in this course take finished blades and attach handles to come up with finished knives.
- **Damascus Steel.** This course prepares participants to produce high-quality Damascus blades.
- **Folding Blades.** This one-week course covers the basics of folding knife construction. Students learn to make both locking and nonlocking blades.
- **Bladesmithing Lab.** Students take on special projects while working with instructors and one another.

Since courses are offered on a noncredit basis, students need not worry about grades. Those who complete courses receive certificates indicating they have earned continuing education units.

It is possible to learn this craft without attending any formal classes. Some people learn the craft of bladesmithing as employees or apprentices of experienced knife makers. A good source of information about this craft is the American Bladesmith Society. Membership in this group is open to anyone interested in bladesmithing, including working knife makers, collectors, and others. The society publishes a quarterly newsletter and sponsors a certification program that can lead to the designation of Master Smith for those who proceed to the highest levels of this intriguing craft.

Bladesmiths sell their products to knife collectors, hunters, and others who appreciate knives of high quality. Workers in plants that manufacture knives and related products tend to use less-specialized skills, instead relying on a more mechanized process.

For more information, contact:

American Bladesmith Society
PO Box 1481
Cypress, TX 77410
www.americanbladesmith.com

American Knife and Tool Institute
22 Vista View Lane
Cody, WY 82414
www.akti.org

Canadian Knifemakers Guild
Rural Route #3
Bridgewater, NS B4V 2W2
Canada
www.ckg.org

National Ornamental Metal Museum
374 Metal Museum Drive
Memphis, TN 38106
www.metalmuseum.org

Professional Knifemakers Association
2905 North Montana Avenue, Suite 30027
Helena, MT 59601
www.proknifemakers.com

School of Bladesmithing
Texarkana College
Evening and Continuing Education Division
2500 North Robison Road
Texarkana, TX 75501
www.americanblade.com

Related Careers

In addition to the careers previously discussed in this chapter, a variety of other occupations involve similar skills. Some, while they involve working with one's hands to create or repair different types of shiny products, might be considered more within the realm of manufacturing or production than the artsy side of crafts. At any rate, these and many other career possibilities hold promise for dexterous types everywhere.

- **Machinists** produce precision parts of metal or plastic. They build new items from printed designs or their own plans, duplicate existing objects, or make precision repairs.
- **Ironworkers** build steel or iron frameworks for buildings or other structures. Some specialize in ornamental work, such as producing wrought iron building parts or furniture.
- **Welders** use heat or other special processes to join metals together. Some work in heavy industries, such as ship-building or building construction. Others use welding processes to make sculpture or pursue more artistic endeavors.
- **Sheet-metal workers** install, produce, or repair sheet-metal products ranging from storage buildings to outdoor signs. Some work for large construction companies. Others run their own businesses, installing aluminum siding or providing other services.
- **Tool-and-die makers** perform work much like that of machinists but at a more advanced level. They produce machine parts and other metal items with an extremely high level of precision.
- **Solderers** use techniques similar to welders, working with small items, such as the internal components of electronic equipment. Their work requires the same kind of patience and attention to detail as many other crafts.
- **Pewtersmiths** work like silversmiths or goldsmiths. But instead of using these precious metals, they use pewter, an alloy of tin and copper.
- **Chain makers** build everything from fine chains used for ornamental purposes to heavier chains designed for industrial uses. Some operate special machines for making chains, while others work by hand.

- **Engravers** add lettering to jewelry, plaques, and other items. Once a process done exclusively by hand, engraving now may also be done through computerized methods. In either case, a continuing demand exists for skilled engravers.
- **Trophy assemblers** put together trophies and plaques. Often, they work with products that have been previously manufactured, providing the finishing touches of assembly and sometimes engraving. While some trophy assemblers work as employees in factories or businesses selling trophies, others operate their own small businesses. In fact, trophy assembly can be an attractive home-based business.

Further Reading

Once you become interested in a specific craft area related to jewelry, precious metals, or other materials, it will be helpful to read specialized information on the subject. The following books and magazines may be of interest.

Books

Barney, Richard W., and Robert W. Loveless. *How to Make Knives*. Krause Publications, 1995.

Baskins, Don. *Well-Shod: A Horseshoeing Guide for Owners and Farriers*. Western Horseman, Incorporated, 2004.

Dismore, Heather, and Tammy Powley. *Jewelry Making and Beading for Dummies*. JohnWiley and Sons, 2004.

Goddard, Wayne. *Wayne Goddard's $50 Knife Shop: Learn to Make Wire Damascus, Build Your Own Tools, Create Beautiful Knives*. KP Books, 2001.

Haab, Sherri. *Designer Style Jewelry: Techniques and Projects for Elegant Designs from Classic to Retro*. Watson-Guptill Publications, 2004.

Krupenia, Deborah; Jessica Wrobel; and Tammy Powley. *The Art of Making Jewelry*. Advanced Global Distribution, 2005.

Lake, Ron; Frank Centofante; and Wayne Clay. *How to Make Folding Knives: A Step-by-Step How-To*. Krause Publications, 1995.

Levine, Bernard R., and Bud Lang, ed. *Levine's Guide to Knives and Their Values: The Complete Book of Knife Collecting*. Krause Publications, 2001.

McCreight, Tim. *Jewelry Making: Techniques for Metal*. Dover Publications, 2005.

Pavelka, Lisa. *Elegant Gifts in Polymer Clay*. North Light Books, 2004.

Peterson, Irene From. *Silver Wire Jewelry: Projects to Coil, Braid and Knit*. Sterling Publishing Company, 2005.

Persico, Jayne, and Stuart Goldman. *Innovative Adornments: An Introduction to Fused Glass and Wire Jewelry*. Wardell Publications, 2005.

Watson, Aldren A. *The Blacksmith: Ironworker and Farrier*. W.W. Norton and Company, 2000.

Wiseman, Nancie. *Crochet with Wire*. Interweave Press, 2005.

Magazines

Blade Magazine
Krause Publications
700 East State Street
Iola, WI 54990
www.blademag.com

Bladesmith's Journal
Hoffman Publications
PO Box 1699
Washington, MO 63090
www.blacksmithsjournal.com

Knife World
PO Box 3395i
Knoxville, TN 37927
www.knifeworld.com

Knives Illustrated
Y-Visionary Publishing
265 South Anita Drive, Suite 120
Orange, CA 92868
www.knivesillustrated.com

Lapidary Journal
300 Chesterfield Parkway, Suite 100
Malvern, PA 19355
www.lapidaryjournal.com

CHAPTER FOUR

Glass, Clay, and Things on Display

Most of the careers described in earlier chapters deal primarily with wood and metal. But those two materials represent just a fraction of the media with which craftspeople can work. Glass, clay, wax, and flowers, among others, also provide creative people with challenging working material. This chapter takes a look at several fascinating career possibilities based on working with these and related materials.

Stained Glass Artist

Have you ever caught your breath in awe at the beauty of an intricate stained glass window as it catches the morning sunlight? If so, you're among the many admirers of stained glass.

Stained glass is usually associated with churches, and rightly so. The huge cathedrals of the Middle Ages gave artisans the chance to develop their craft to perfection. They set a standard that has held up for centuries.

While the use of stained glass may never again reach the pinnacle of prestige it had in the Middle Ages, it has nevertheless survived to the present day. In fact, stained glass has enjoyed something of a resurgence in recent years. Modern-day churches still provide a demand for stained glass windows as new sanctuaries are built or existing structures expanded.

The skill of making stained glass has become something of a rarity, but those who work in this area also find a demand for other products such as lamps, wall decorations, holiday ornaments, and sun catchers, which are small panels designed for placement on ordinary windows. Some makers of stained glass specialize in windows, lamps, or door panels. Others make small trinkets or gifts.

Experienced professionals recommend that newcomers to this field take one or two primary approaches to learning the craft. One is to locate an experienced craftsperson and offer to serve as an apprentice. The other is to enroll in classes taught at craft schools, summer workshops, or other educational programs.

For instance, the Rhode Island School of Design offers a four-year program in working with glass that includes a course in stained glass.

For more information on this or other schools that offer classes on working with stained glass, or about organizations related to the craft, contact:

Association of Stained Glass Lamp Artists
5070 Cromwell Drive NW
Gig Harbor, WA 98335
www.asgla.com

Creative Glass Center of America
Wheaton Village
1501 Glasstown Road
Millville, NJ 08332
www.wheatonvillage.org

Fletcher Farm School for the Arts and Crafts
611 Route 103 South
Ludlow, VT 05149
www.fletcherfarm.com

Glass Art Association of Canada
1507 Westall Avenue
Victoria, BC V8T 2G6
Canada
www.glassartcanada.ca

Glass Art Society
3131 Western Avenue, Suite 414
Seattle, WA 98121
www.glassart.org

Rhode Island School of Design
Two College Street
Providence, RI 02903
www.risd.edu

Stained Glass Association of America
10009 East Sixty-Second Street
Raytown, MO 64133
www.stainedglass.org

Glassblower

Glassblowers produce some of the most beautiful items known to humankind. After all, glass itself, with its ability to diffract and reflect light, is inherently pretty. But when this already attractive material takes on the delicate shapes and symmetry made possible by glassblowing techniques, the results can be breathtaking. Vases, tumblers, sculptures, Christmas tree ornaments, and many other decorative and functional items are produced by glassblowers.

Blowing glass is a highly specialized craft. Those who master it hold creative, demanding jobs. Some work in factories that produce specialty glassware. Others operate as one-person businesses. Some teach their skills in schools or workshop settings.

In the traditional method of blowing glass, the craftsperson dips a long blowpipe, made of iron, into a mixture of molten glass, then lifts the pipe and blows into the tube while rotating a glob of hot glass retrieved from the molten mixture. The result is a hollow glass object that has been shaped according to the desires of the glassblower.

Today, even though mass production and other aspects of modern technology have made glass production a large-scale endeavor, there is still a place for manual glassblowing. Modern consumers love to purchase handblown glass. In fact, people will often pay a premium for such items.

A visit to the Blenko glass factory near Milton, West Virginia, provides a fascinating look at the craft of glassblowing. Here, visitors can watch working artisans as they produce blown-glass products. The slow and careful process of creating a vase, for instance, provides visitors with an inside look at the painstaking work involved. The factory also includes an outlet shop where finished pieces are sold.

Several qualities are needed to pursue this highly specialized craft area. Chief among them are patience, an eye for proportion, stamina, and creativity. A tolerance for heat is also required. Most craftspeople in this field share an intense desire for perfection.

Because of its specialized nature, glassblowing is not taught as widely as are some other crafts. Some craft schools and summer programs include courses in glassblowing. An unusually diverse selection of courses is available at the Pilchuck Glass School in Seattle, Washington. Courses vary from session to session, with typical examples including:

- Beginning Glassblowing
- Hot Glass: Historical Preferences, Modern Techniques
- Goblets: Form and Function
- Master Glassblowing
- Glassblowing: Sculpture from Natural Sources

- Stained Glass—Up Close and Public
- The Road to the Mold

For more information, contact:

Pilchuck Glass School
430 Yale Avenue North
Seattle, WA 98109
www.pilchuck.com

Potter or Ceramic Artist

Long before glass was invented, people made clay pottery. Ancient civilizations learned to shape jars, pots, vases, and even writing tablets out of clay. Though other materials have largely replaced clay in the creation of these objects, there has always been a place for the work of potters and ceramic artists who can shape clay into functional or artistic forms.

Today, potters and ceramic artists produce a variety of products, ranging from simple vases to delicate figurines. Some work primarily with earthenware or stoneware, both of which are relatively heavy materials. Others specialize in working with porcelain, which is more delicate. Their methods of making pottery include using slabs or coils of clay, molds, or a potter's wheel. The craft includes not just shaping the object to be made but also techniques such as glazing and firing.

Some potters work full-time at their craft. Others pursue it on a part-time basis. In either case, a serious potter must invest in the right equipment. It is not unusual to spend $2,000 or more for a wheel, kiln, and related materials.

Craftspeople who do make this a full-time career are in the minority. Some make a go of it by specializing in more expensive items or by mass-producing a basic, popular line of products such as mugs or cups. Others combine their work with teaching. Some potters work for firms that produce dishware or other pottery or porcelain products instead of operating their own businesses.

Techniques for working with clay are widely taught. Community colleges and the continuing education divisions of four-year colleges and universities often offer courses and seminars to anyone who is interested. Most of these offerings are taught on a noncredit basis.

Craft schools, many of which operate only in the summer, also offer classes in pottery and related areas. An example is Haystack Mountain School of Crafts in Deer Isle, Maine. Each summer, this school offers several classes on working with clay lasting one to three weeks each. Some focus on wheel-thrown pottery, while others cover hand-building techniques. Related topics, such as painting ceramic objects, are also offered.

Peters Valley Craft Center in Layton, New Jersey, is another school offering classes in ceramics. Typical summer workshop titles include:

- Form, Function, and Surface
- The Dimension of Color
- Functional Pots
- Raku Firing: Kilns and Glazes

For more information, contact:

American Art Pottery Association
PO Box 834
Westport, MA 02790
www.amartpot.org

Canadian Crafts Federation
170 Bedford Road, Suite 300
Toronto, ON M5R 2K9
Canada
www.canadiancraftsfederation.ca

Haystack Mountain School of Crafts
PO Box 518
Deer Isle, ME 04627
www.haystack-mtn.org

Peters Valley Craft Center
19 Kuhn Road
Layton, NJ 07851
www.pvcrafts.org

Potters Guild of British Columbia
1359 Cartright Street, Granville Island
Vancouver, BC V6H 3R7
Canada
www.bcpotters.com

. . . .

Floral Designer

"A thing of beauty is a joy forever," the poet John Keats noted. Of course, that was before the days of FTD! While flowers may not last forever, there is certainly no doubt that flowers bring joy as well as other desired effects. Well-designed floral arrangements can thrill brides, surprise spouses, comfort the sick, or convey a message of sympathy.

With the value people place on flowers, it is not surprising that the floral industry is a large and thriving one. Within this multi-faceted business are not only jobs in sales, agriculture, and other areas, but also opportunities for those with an inclination toward crafts. Specifically, the job of floral designer offers great promise for people with an eye for beauty and a creative flair.

Floral designers have a wider range of career opportunities than do followers of some other crafts due to the immense popularity of flowers. This multibillion-dollar industry has room for independent floral designers or florists, those employed by retail flower shops, and various related workers, including cut-flower processors, salespeople, interior landscapers, and managers in retail or wholesale establishments.

Although on-the-job training is possible, most floral designers today receive some type of formal education. Many vocational schools, trade schools, and community colleges offer programs in floral design or the related areas of floriculture or horticulture. Some of these programs take two years to complete, while others can be finished in a year or less. A catalog of schools offering a variety of programs is available from the Society of American Florists. A nearby community college or vocational school may also be a possibility if you would like to explore this career area.

People with disabilities may be interested in a special program that supports the hiring of the disabled in the horticulture field. This national referral network has placed more than one thousand people in jobs in the floral industry and related fields. For more details, contact the American Horticultural Therapy Association.

For more information, contact:

American Horticultural Therapy Association
3570 East Twelfth Avenue
Denver, CO 80206
www.ahta.org

Canadian Horticultural Therapy Association
100 Westmount Road
Guelph, ON N1H 5H8
Canada
www.chta.ca

National Junior Horticulture Association
15 Railroad Avenue
Homer City, PA 15748
www.njha.org

North American Horticultural Supply Association
100 North Twentieth Street, Fourth Floor
Philadelphia, PA 19103
www.nahsa.org

Society of American Florists
1601 Duke Street
Alexandria, VA 22314
www.safnow.org

....

Picture Framer

What if you're not the most artistic person in the world, but the idea of a crafts career appeals to you? One occupation worth considering is that of professional picture framer. This is not to say that picture framers lack talent; on the contrary, this craft provides much in the way of creative challenge. On the other hand, almost anyone can take a shot at this field. The main requirements are patience and enthusiasm. An eye for proportion is also helpful, as is an appreciation for color, contrast, and texture. And as with virtually every craft area, the ability to work with your hands is needed. Most people can develop their abilities in these areas, so career possibilities are wide open in this field.

What do picture framers do? That may sound like a silly question. They frame pictures, of course! But actually, the job is more complex than it might seem at first glance. It involves choosing materials, making special borders called mats (or mattes), assembling frames, cutting glass, and handling other tasks necessary for protecting and displaying pictures. These pictures could be photographs, paintings, or drawings. Picture framers also work with a wide range of other items, including diplomas, certificates, rare documents, maps, newspaper clippings, collages, and needle craft. Framers also work with objects that are not as flat as pictures and documents. For example, they might construct frameworks or displays for coin collections, arrowheads, or medallions.

The world of picture framing goes hand in hand with that of the visual arts. Some painters, for instance, learn to make their own frames, then go on to provide this service for others. In the process, they develop skills in a second field, which enhances their ability to produce income.

Some picture framers build working relationships with artists in which they not only provide frames but also help market the finished product. They might operate an art gallery as an adjunct to their framing services.

Many picture framers are self-employed or operate their own small businesses. Others work for art galleries, museums, or private companies that manufacture frames.

Running a framing shop can be one of the most promising ways to combine a crafts-related career with a small business that appeals to a broad segment of the public. These shops serve not just the artistic community, but everyone from hobbyists to doting grandparents anxious to display huge color photos of the cutest grandchildren in the universe. As such, they provide a way for the competent framer to build and operate a successful business.

Working as an employee in a frame shop or gallery represents one of the best ways to get started in this field. Here, experienced framers are sometimes willing to train a part-time employee or apprentice. Working with an experienced picture framer can provide perhaps the best introduction to the craft.

Other approaches are to take classes or seminars on picture framing, to read books on the subject, or to view videotapes on basic framing techniques. All are available through the Professional Picture Framers Association (PPFA), an organization with over three thousand members from the United States and Canada. It provides a variety of services of interest to anyone committed to picture framing as a professional endeavor.

Newcomers to the field will be especially interested in the various instructional opportunities offered through the association.

These include seminars that are offered throughout the United States and Canada and are open to nonmembers as well as to PPFA members. Examples of seminar topics include:

- Beginning Mat Cutting
- Object Box Framing
- Conservation Framing
- Gallery Presentation and Display

Also of special interest is an association bookstore that provides books and training videos. Not only are they easily ordered by mail, telephone, or online, but prices are discounted for members. Examples of videotapes include *The Basics of Picture Framing* and *The Basics of Mat Cutting and Decoration*, both by Vivian Kistler, as well as other tapes on topics ranging from conservation framing to French matting.

Another appealing service is a special program for certifying professional picture framers. This provides a helpful way to recognize professional skills. For more information, contact:

Professional Picture Framers Association
300 Picture Place
Jackson, MI 49201
www.ppfa.com

Candle Maker

A craft area that has been making something of a comeback in recent years is candle making. Used purely for decoration or burned as an alternative to modern electric lights, candles are popular items with people from a variety of backgrounds.

"For romantics, candles are always in," says Chris Saunders, a Virginia candle maker. He makes candles of various sizes and configurations, selling them at crafts fairs and by consignment in shops. "Candles are great for people who believe in a return to the basics," Saunders says. "You can produce them in quantity, or you can consider each one a work of art."

To learn about the craft, Saunders suggests contacting a working craftsperson and learning firsthand. Individual practice and experimentation are essential. Although there is plenty of room for creativity, this area is one where beginners can learn quickly.

Working candle makers and others interested in the field belong to the International Guild of Candle Artisans. This group produces a newsletter called *The Candlelighter*, sponsors conferences, and even operates a hotline to provide tips on problems candle makers encounter in their work. Also of note are workshops the group holds that feature instruction in candle making techniques. For more information, contact:

International Guild of Candle Artisans
1640 Greenfield
Fremont, NE 68025
www.igca.net

National Candle Association
1156 Fifteenth Street NW, Suite 900
Washington, DC 20005
www.candles.org

Related Careers

In addition to the careers profiled in this chapter, a wide range of occupations deal with glass, clay, or other materials. Following is a brief listing of some of them.

- **Fused glass artists** form and shape glass in kilns. They construct everything from cups and bowls to abstract sculptures.

- **Glaziers** cut and install window glass. While this work falls more within the area of construction than that of handicrafts, it requires skill and precision akin to that needed by other craftspeople who work with glass.
- **Glass decorators** use painting or other techniques to add designs to glass products. This may be done by hand or through automated processes.
- **Porcelain ware designers** create the designs that other workers follow in producing dishware and related products. Their work revolves more around the creation of new designs than the actual production of pieces in quantity.
- **Optical technicians** and others who work with optical products create lenses, optical mirrors, and related objects. This work can range from the routine production of eyeglass lenses to highly individualized work such as grinding and polishing lenses or mirrors for telescopes.

Further Reading

Books

Atkin, Jacqui. *Handbuilt Pottery Techniques Revealed: The Secrets of Handbuilding Shown in Unique Cutaway Photography.* Barron's Educational Series, 2004.

Browning, Marie. *Totally Cool Polymer Clay Projects.* Sterling Publishing Company, 2004.

Duval, Elizabeth. *Beyond the Basics: Mosaics.* Sterling Publishing Company, 2004.

Gault, Rosette. *Paper Clay.* University of Pennsylvania Press, 2004.

Hamer, Janet, and Frank Hamer. *The Potter's Dictionary of Materials and Techniques.* University of Pennsylvania Press, 2004.

Hopper, Robin. *Making Marks: Discovering the Ceramic Surface.* Krause Publications, 2004.

Itabashi, Hiromi; Naoki Kawabuchi; and Roppo Tamura. *Building Your Own Kiln: Three Japanese Potters Give Advice and Instructions.* Kodan-Sha America, 2004.

Peterson, Susan. *The Craft and Art of Clay: A Complete Potter's Handbook.* Overlook Hardcover, 2003.

Pozo, Angelica. *Making and Installing Handmade Tiles.* Sterling Publishing Company, 2005.

Rhodes, Daniel. *Pottery Form.* Dover Publications, 2004.

Spear, Sue. *Candle Making in a Weekend.* North Light Books, 1999.

Vincentelli, Moira. *Women Potters: Transforming Traditions.* Rutgers University Press, 2004.

Warshaw, Josie. *Handbuilding Pottery: Practical Art Handbook.* Anness Publishing, 2005.

Watkins, James C., and Paul Andrew Wandless. *Alternative Kilns and Firing Techniques.* Sterling Publishing Company, 2004.

Wells, Krista. *Polymer Clay Mosaics.* Sterling Publishing Company, 2004.

Magazines

Ceramics Monthly
735 Ceramic Place, Suite 100
Westerville, OH 43081
www.ceramicsmonthly.org

Contemporary Canadian Glass
Glass Art Association of Canada
1507 Westall Avenue
Victoria, BC V8T 2G6
Canada
www.glassartcanada.ca

DECOR Magazine
1801 Park 270 Drive
Maryland Heights, MO 63146
www.decormagazine.com

Journal of the Glass Art Society
Glass Art Society
3131 Western Avenue, Suite 414
Seattle, WA 98121
www.glassart.org

Stained Glass Quarterly
Stained Glass Association of America
10009 East Sixty-Second Street
Raytown, MO 64133
www.stainedglass.org

CHAPTER FIVE

Leather and Lace

re you passionate about leather? After all, you don't need to be
a biker to appreciate the soft feel and rich smell of new
leather. Or are you more of a soft-fabric type? The delicate
beauty of handcrafted textiles can be hard to beat.

Whatever your fabric preferences, a variety of craft areas
address them. In fact, the creation of clothing, rugs, quilts, and
other items represents one of the more diverse of existing craft
areas. Craftspeople who can sew, weave, design clothing, or perform related work often find substantial demand for their products. By the same token, crafty types can find many rewards by
working in this area.

Leather Artisan

Craftspeople who work with leather provide products that are
useful, long lasting, and often quite attractive. In an age dominated by synthetic materials and mass-produced clothing, these
products appeal to the growing popularity of handmade, individualized items. Since leather is widely used by both men and
women, the market for finely crafted goods is a large one.

Successful leather artisans are found in both rural and urban
areas. Typically, they begin working with leather on a part-time
basis. Some continue as part-time artisans, while others make
the transition to full-time careers in crafting and selling leather
products.

Creativity, persistence, and the ability to meet the needs of a variety of customers are necessary traits for leather artisans who wish to succeed. For example, one customer might want a leather rifle case, while another might be interested in items to be used in motorcycling. A willingness to travel is also helpful, since it might be necessary to travel to crafts fairs and stores or attend leather conventions.

As with any craft, there are some shortcomings. One is that leather is a rather expensive raw material, thus items that are made but not sold can tie up a good deal of money. Another occasional problem is protest by some animal rights activists. Since leather comes from the hides of cows and a variety of more exotic animals, those who work with leather can become targets of criticism from activists. This situation is generally not as controversial as it is with fur, but it can come up. Artisans who work with leather generally learn noncombative responses to use if criticized about this issue.

Some working craftspeople in this field belong to professional groups of those with similar interests.

For more information, contact:

International Federation of Leather Guilds
   (in summer)
3117 Babette Drive
Southport, IN 46227
or
   (in winter)
7318 Highway 441 SE
Okeechobee, FL 34974
www.ifolg.org

International Internet Leathercrafters' Guild
www.iilg.org

Weaver

If you want to stick with a traditional craft, it would be hard to beat weaving. Weavers carry on a practice that has continued throughout the world for thousands of years. Today's weavers provide an alternative to the high-volume, industrialized processes with which most cloth-based materials are produced. The beautiful patterns of a hand-woven tapestry, for example, stand in stark contrast to mass-produced cloth created through assembly-line production methods.

For those with the right combination of skill and patience, weaving can provide a productive career area. Accomplished weavers create not just functional items such as shawls or rugs but also highly prized works of art.

Learning the basics of weaving often means working on a two-harness loom to create a rug or tapestry. Beginning weavers first choose the colors with which they plan to work and decide which weaving techniques they would like to master. They may study drawings of weaving techniques, learn to use the loom, and begin working on their initial weaving projects.

The downside of weaving, from a career viewpoint, is that it is difficult to produce and sell enough pieces to earn a living, given the methodical nature of the weaving process. Weavers can make a living, however, thanks not just to individual productivity but also to the value many customers place in hand-woven material. As with many other products in the arts and crafts, the work of an accomplished weaver can fetch excellent prices. With skill and persistence, it is possible to make weaving a part-time or full-time occupation.

Weavings of first-rate craftspeople are popular items for decorating offices, government buildings, and homes. Weavers sell their products through galleries, arts and crafts fairs, special arrangements with merchandisers, and their own marketing efforts.

A good source of information is the Handweavers Guild of America. A local fine arts center, crafts center, or college continuing education program may also offer classes or put you in touch with accomplished weavers. For more information, contact:

Art Institute of Chicago
111 South Michigan Avenue
Chicago, IL 60603
www.artic.edu

Berea College
CPO Box 2142
Berea, KY 40404
www.berea.edu

Crossnore School
PO Box 249
Crossnore, NC 28615
www.crossnoreschool.org

Fiber Arts Center of the Northwest
PO Box 1262
Rochester, WA 98579
www.fiberartscenter.org

The Guild of Canadian Weavers
19 Klondike Road
Whitehorse, YK Y1A 3L8
Canada
www.the-gcw.org

Handweavers Guild of America
1255 Buford Highway, Suite 211
Sewanee, GA 30024
www.weavespindye.org

Handweaving Museum and Arts Center
314 John Street
Clayton, NY 13624
www.hm-ac.org

Haystack Mountain School of Crafts
PO Box 518
Deer Isle, ME 04627
www.haystack-mtn.org

Haywood Community College
185 Freedlander Drive
Clyde, NC 28721
www.haywood.edu

Oregon College of Art and Craft
8425 Southwest Barnes Road
Portland, OR 97225
www.ocac.edu

Springwater Fiber Workshop
808 North Fairfax Street
Alexandria, VA 22314
www.springwaterfiber.org

Weaving Arts Studio
101 South Babcock Street
Tellico Plains, TN 37385
www.weavingschool.com

Weaving Southwest
216 B Paseo del Pueblo Norte
Taos, NM 87571
www.weavingsouthwest.com

. . . .

Quilter

Some craft areas hold special appeal because they continue the legacy of the past. As with weaving, this is certainly true of quilting, one of the most popular of craft areas. The days of the quilting bee may be virtually over, but people of all ages still love the unique appeal of quilted materials.

While the major item of interest in the field is probably the traditional quilt to be used as a bed covering, those skilled in crafting produce a variety of other materials. Examples include place mats, runners, coasters, table centers, and wall hangings.

Making quilts by hand takes great patience. The finished work is often coveted by customers and may fetch high prices. From a business viewpoint, the difficulty is reconciling the many hours it takes to produce fine work with the need to keep costs low enough for customers to afford.

An alternative to making quilts entirely by hand is machine quilting. This process is considerably faster but still produces beautiful work. Some quilters learn both processes to increase their capacity while not abandoning traditional methods.

To learn more about quilting, consult one of the many books available on the subject. (Several are listed at the end of this chapter.) Or take a class or talk with someone in your area who is active in quilting. Also check out these organizations:

American Quilter's Society
PO Box 3290
Paducah, KY 42002
www.americanquilter.com

Canadian Quilters' Association
1150 River Road
Manotick, ON K4M 1B4
Canada
www.canadianquilters.com

The Quilters Hall of Fame
PO Box 681
Marion, IN 46952
www.quiltershalloffame.org

. . . .

Doll Maker

Another very popular craft is making dolls. This is an area dear to the hearts of a surprisingly large number of people. Dolls are not just for children, if this craft is any indicator. To the contrary, the work of doll makers is of interest to a wide range of customers, including collectors, parents, grandparents, and doll enthusiasts of all ages.

Those who make dolls work with a wide range of materials. Some create finely wrought figures of porcelain. Some doll makers use wood, plastic, or other durable materials. Still others fashion dolls out of cloth, corn cobs, or whatever else might work. Doll makers also specialize in a variety of subjects, including clowns, mechanical dolls, and dolls dressed in period costumes.

A good source of information about doll making is the Doll Artisan Guild, headquartered in Oneonta, New York. Members of this organization receive six issues per year of *The Doll Artisan* (a magazine that includes pull-out worksheets for doll-making projects), enjoy discounts from manufacturers, and compete for awards based on their work. The group also sponsors conventions, doll-making seminars, and opportunities to become certified at several levels of ability.

Several other groups also serve the needs of doll makers. For more information, contact:

Academy of American Doll Artists
26 Rachael Circle
Goffstown, NH 03045
www.aadadoll.org

Canadian Doll Artists Association
62 Settlers Way
Kemptville, ON K0G 1J0
Canada
www.dollartists.ca

Doll Artisan Guild
118 Commerce Road
PO Box 1113
Oneonta, NY 13820
www.dollartisanguild.com

Doll Costumers Guild
5042 Wilshire Boulevard, PMB 573
Los Angeles, CA 90036
www.dollcostumersguild.com

International Doll Makers Association
25146 Maplewood Drive
Athens, AL 35613
www.idmadolls.com

International Foundation of Doll Makers
PO Box 120187
Clermont, FL 34712
www.ifdm.org

Original Doll Artist Council of America
www.odaca.org

Basket Maker

Basket makers also practice a craft that goes back thousands of years. Remember the story of Moses floating at the edge of the Nile River? The boat holding the infant was actually a basket.

Throughout history, craftspeople from almost every culture have made and used baskets. Today's basket makers use the same kinds of techniques that have existed for centuries, with the added benefit of new raw materials, paints, and other coverings.

Materials used to make baskets include strips of wood or bark, grass, and various fibers ranging from wool and cotton to synthetic fibers. The major attributes needed to produce baskets of good quality are patience, steady hands, and skill developed through practice.

The Arrowmont School of Arts and Crafts in Gatlinburg, Tennessee, is one school that teaches classes in basket making. For example, one course called Rattan Wicker Basketry covers the construction of traditional wicker baskets using rattan—the stems of any of several climbing palms. Topics of discussion include wicker weaving, making lids and handles, and dealing with color.

Many other schools also offer seminars or short courses in basketry. Check with a nearby community college or adult education program to identify available courses in your area. For more information about classes offered in basket making, contact:

Arrowmont School of Arts and Crafts
556 Parkway
Gatlinburg, TN 37738
www.arrowmont.org

Fashion Designer

A major career area for people with the right artistic bent is the design of dresses and other clothing. This can range from a home-based business, in which you design and sew clothing for customers within your own community, to working as a designer for a major apparel firm.

Clothing design offers a wide range of opportunities for part-time or full-time employment. Some examples of career possibilities in this area are as follows:

- designing wedding gowns for a clothing manufacturer
- designing and creating wedding gowns through your own home-based business
- designing costumes for plays, movies, or television
- providing custom dress design services for specialty stores or boutiques
- operating your own tailoring business
- providing customized tailoring services for men's clothing stores or department stores
- designing and setting up window displays for department stores or clothing stores
- working as a milliner for a hat company
- providing alteration services for cleaners, clothing stores, or other establishments
- designing or producing clothing for specialized groups such as infants or small children

Although it is possible to pursue a career in fashion or clothing design based on your own talent and experimentation, it is often helpful to pursue specialized training. One approach is to work as an apprentice or assistant to an experienced designer. Another is to enroll in classes offered by a school that offers fashion design or related programs.

One example is the Fashion Institute of Technology (FIT) in New York City. Here, students may choose from a number of programs and options related to fashion design. At FIT, students pursue either an associate's degree or a bachelor's degree. They take courses such as the following:

- Accessories Design
- Advertising and Marketing Communications
- Advertising Design
- Business Enterprise
- Computer Animation and Interactive Media

- Cosmetics and Fragrance Marketing
- Display and Exhibit Design
- Fabric Styling
- Fashion Design
- Fashion Merchandising Management
- Graphic Design
- Illustration
- Interior Design
- International Trade and Marketing
- Marketing: Fashion and Related Industries
- Millinery
- Packaging Design
- Patternmaking Technology
- Restoration
- Tailoring Techniques
- Textile/Surface Design
- Textile Development and Marketing
- Toy Design

Do you have to take courses in all of these areas? Not necessarily, but obviously a job applicant with such training will have an advantage over one who has no special training in fashion design. On the other hand, many of the concepts taught in formal courses can be picked up through related job experience. If you are lucky enough to sign on with an experienced designer, or if you start out working alone but do plenty of reading, studying, and practicing in the field, it is possible to get started in fashion design without a great deal of formal instruction.

A career in fashion design has its pros and cons. On the negative side, this is an extremely competitive field. On the positive side, designing new fashions offers the potential of business success along with the fun of creating new designs. This is not a field for everyone, but it is one that can be highly rewarding for the right crafty person. For more information, contact:

Fashion Institute of Technology
Seventh Avenue at Twenty-Seventh Street
New York, NY 10001
www.fitnyc.edu

Bookbinder

The skills of sewing and cutting are not confined to making clothes, baskets, or other household items. A related but very different area is the binding of books. With all the high-tech equipment used in today's publishing industry, you might think that bookbinding is an outdated craft. Not true!

Books are fragile. Older volumes may begin to fall apart due to extensive use, age, or a combination of the two. Yet they may be worth saving. In fact, many old books are considered valuable by collectors, professors, libraries, and others. In repairing books, bookbinders extend the useful life of the volumes. In addition, newly published books targeted to limited audiences may require hand binding instead of the mass-production techniques used for the latest bestseller. As a result of demands for both kinds of work, a continuing need exists for skilled bookbinders.

Employers of bookbinders include binderies, university publishers and libraries, and custom shops specializing in bookbinding, publishing, or related services. Some bookbinders also go the small-business route and operate their own businesses.

Due to the specialized nature of bookbinding, some type of training is necessary to get started in this field. Some schools offer continuing education classes or summer workshops, and a few offer more extensive training.

A school offering a full-fledged program in this field is North Bennet Street School in Boston. Here, students learn bookbinding through a two-year program that includes training in the unique vocabulary and techniques of bookbinding, followed by intensive hands-on experience in repairing books from the nineteenth and twentieth centuries as well as working with new books. Students attend small classes (average class size is twelve) for forty weeks each year, meeting daily from 8 A.M. to 2 P.M. Along with classroom instruction, they go on field trips and attend special lectures and demonstrations. The main component of the program, however, is extensive bench work.

Another school teaching bookbinding is the Penland School of Crafts in North Carolina. Along with classes in other areas, courses in bookbinding are offered. One course covers basic binding and box-making skills with work progressing toward more complicated structures and ideas. Student projects range from Ethiopian-style bindings with leather cases to contemporary accordion-style flip books and creative boxes.

If you are unable to attend a school of this type, it may be possible to learn bookbinding through an arrangement with an experienced craftsperson. Through a formal apprenticeship or informal, on-the-job training, a diligent worker can learn the techniques of this field. To succeed, you will need patience, good hand-eye coordination, and other skills not unlike those of many other craft areas. A love of books is also a great asset. In fact, a dedicated bookbinder regards books the way a jeweler treasures diamonds.

With a deep respect for the value of books, an eye for beauty, and a willingness to work patiently, skilled bookbinders provide important work. For more information about careers in bookbinding, contact:

Book Manufacturers' Institute
Two Armund Beach Drive, Suite 1B
Palm Coast, FL 32137
www.bmibook.com

Canadian Bookbinders and Book Artists Guild
60 Atlantic Avenue, Suite 112
Toronto, ON M6K 1X9
Canada
www.cbbag.ca

Guild of Book Workers
521 Fifth Avenue
New York, NY 10175
http://palimpsest.stanford.edu/byorg/gbw

North Bennet Street School
39 North Bennet Street
Boston, MA 02113
www.nbss.org

Penland School of Crafts
PO Box 37
Penland, NC 28765
www.penland.org

The Center for Book Arts
28 West Twenty-Seventh Street, Third Floor
New York, NY 10001
www.centerforbookarts.org

Related Careers

Occupations related to those discussed in this chapter include the following:

- **Fur designers** create designs for coats, hats, and other items made of animal fur. Their work is similar to that of fashion designers but with a more narrow range of working materials.
- **Lace and textile restorers** work primarily for museums. They repair and restore old clothing, linens, and other related items of historical value.
- **Gift wrappers** work primarily for retail stores but may also operate their own businesses. They use skills not greatly different from those of designers. They choose color

combinations and designs and wrap packages as creatively as possible.

- **Mannequin decorators** create store displays by dressing and posing mannequins. They exercise creativity in trying to catch the attention of customers by coming up with interesting or attractive clothing combinations.
- **Furniture upholsterers** add the fabric coverings to the frameworks of sofas, chairs, and other types of furniture. Some specialize in working with new furniture, while others focus on reupholstering older furniture.
- **Saddlers** perform the highly specialized job of making or repairing saddles used in riding horses. They may also sell saddles made by others. Some saddlers also make related products such as stirrups or reins; the latter work can also be performed by harness makers.

Further Reading

Books

Alderman, Sharon. *Mastering Weave Structures: Transforming Ideas into Great Cloth*. Interweave Press, 2004.

Cambras, Joseph. *Complete Book of Bookbinding*. Sterling Publishing Company, 2004.

Garner, Lynne. *Native American Bead Weaving*. Guild of Master Craftsman Publications, 2003.

Lee, Kari. *Gorgeous Leather Crafts: 30 Projects to Stamp, Stencil, Weave & Tool*. Lark, 2003.

Landman, Sylvia Ann. *Make Money Quilting*. Allworth Press, 2005.

Menz, Deb. *Color in Spinning*. Interweave Press, 2005.

Shrader, Valerie Van Arsdale. *Hip Handbags: Creating and Embellishing 40 Great-Looking Bags*. Sterling Publishing Company, 2005.

Stauffer, Jeanne. *Learn to Quilt with Leather.* House of White Birches, 2005.

Stol, Truus, and Janny Roelofsen. *Willow Weaving.* Search Press, 2004.

Taylor, Kathleen. *Yarns to Dye for: Creating Self-Patterning Yarns for Knitting.* Interweave Press, 2004.

Van der Hoogt, Madelyn, ed. *Twill Thrills: 36 Projects in the New Twills.* XRX Books, 2004.

Magazines

American Quilter Magazine
PO Box 3290
Paducah, KY 42002
www.americanquilter.com

Bead & Button Magazine
PO Box 1612
Waukesha, WI 53187
www.beadandbutton.com

Dolls Beautiful
PO Box 1113
Oneonta, NY 13820
www.dollartisanguild.org

Guild of Book Workers Journal
Guild of Book Workers
521 Fifth Avenue
New York, NY 10175
http://palimpsest.stanford.edu/byorg/gbw

Handwoven
Interweave Press
201 East Fourth Street
Loveland, CO 80537
www.interweave.com

Paper Crafts Magazine
14850 Pony Express Road
Bluffdale, UT 84065
www.papercraftsmag.com

PaperWorks
PO Box 9001
Big Sandy, TX 75755
www.paperworksmagazine.com

PieceWork
201 East Fourth Street
Loveland, CO 80537
www.interweave.com

CHAPTER SIX

Graphic Details

Any discussion of crafts careers would be incomplete without a look at the graphic arts. Creating and producing lettering, drawings, and other graphic images is an area rich in possibilities for the crafty person.

Do you enjoy drawing? Painting? Coming up with visual images that in a single glance convey more than a page of words? If so, one of the following careers may be just right for you.

Craft Painter

The distinction between artist and craftsperson is a fuzzy one. In the area of painting, someone who produces lifelike oil paintings of museum quality would probably be called an artist.

Someone else who adds painted illustrations to functional objects would probably be called a craftsperson. For example, one craft technique is painting on the blades of handsaws. Another is applying likenesses of birds or forest animals to rough wood, such as remnants from old barns or fences. Some craftspeople specialize in making decorative pieces from old slates once used for roofing, products that appeal to buyers who covet a token of the past. At the same time, slate makes an attractive material for wall hangings, plaques, clocks, trivets, spoon racks, refrigerator magnets, and desk name blocks, among other items. Surfaces may be decorated with images of flowers, wildlife, farm animals, barns, covered bridges, and other pastoral objects.

Other craft painters work with a variety of media. Many sell their works at crafts fairs or by word of mouth. Some combine their crafts with teaching, running frame shops, or pursuing other crafts.

An advantage of craft painting is that no special training is necessary. Although classes in painting or drawing can be helpful, anyone who has basic abilities in drawing or painting and who can develop products of respectable quality might find this craft of interest.

Sign Painter

Sign painters (or sign writers, if you prefer) design and apply lettering and graphic designs for use in various kinds of signs. They might produce billboards, posters, door and window signs, and other types of messages.

Sign painting can be the major product of a small business or one of many such services provided by a full-service graphics or printing establishment. Sign painters can work as self-employed craftspeople or as employees of graphics firms, outdoor advertising companies, full-service ad agencies, or other types of employers.

Traditionally, the work of sign painters has been done by hand. A typical example would be the application of a person's name on the outside of an office's glass door. Using a brush and paint, the sign painter carefully adds the appropriate lettering. As technology changes, however, much of this work is being accomplished through the use of lettering machines or computerized processes. Sign writers might also employ skills ranging from screen printing to working with gold or silver leaf.

Calligrapher

If you have ever spotted words such as *whereas* or *wherefore* in a modern-day document, or the abbreviation *RSVP* in an invitation, chances are you have seen the work of a calligrapher. Such wording is the staple of formal resolutions, invitations, and similarly printed materials.

Calligraphers produce hand-lettered material for situations in which the appearance of the finished product is of special importance. Invitations, nameplates, resolutions, diplomas, and certificates of merit are just a few examples. In documents such as these, it is the job of the calligrapher to provide attractive lettering, often with the goal of simulating the old-fashioned lettering used in the days before typewriting (let alone word processing and desktop publishing) was commonplace.

A job as a calligrapher is likely to be a part-time one or else a component of a more broad-based career that includes other types of graphic services. By its very nature, calligraphy is a painstakingly slow process, and it is difficult to consistently produce enough finished work to support a full-fledged career. However, some people do succeed at making it a full-time occupation or at combining it with computerized work. They provide services to businesses, government agencies, nonprofit organizations, and individuals.

For the right person, calligraphy can provide highly satisfying work that differs greatly from more mainstream careers. It combines the creativity of the artist with the precision of the craft practitioner. In fact, the term *calligraphy* can be roughly translated from its Greek origins as "beautiful writing." This important element of beauty makes calligraphy stand out from many other occupations.

Working alone or in collaboration with a client, the calligrapher first chooses the style of lettering to be used in any given project. Then, he or she carefully draws each letter using special pens designed to transfer an even flow of ink onto the paper.

A typical task would consist of taking a stack of printed certificates developed to honor a group of employees or volunteers and, one by one, writing in the names of the individual recipients. Other typical projects are producing corporate logos, lettering invitations to special events, or developing place cards for formal dinners.

Some calligraphers go beyond basic lettering to produce artistic works. These can include unusual renditions of lettering in which the letters themselves become a creative art form. Another approach is to add drawings to lettering, producing a combined art form akin to the illustrated manuscripts introduced in medieval times.

Most calligraphers learn their craft through a combination of instruction and individual practice. The instructional end might include a class or two being offered by a community college, a workshop presented during a summer camp or arts and crafts festival, classes offered through a public school system's community education program, or lessons taken from an experienced calligrapher. Another alternative is simply consulting books about calligraphy and mastering the craft independently.

Whatever the means of initial instruction, the bulk of the learning process consists of practicing the appropriate techniques. Like learning to play the piano or successfully shoot free throws in basketball, learning calligraphy means practice, practice, and more practice. Once the basics of this demanding craft have been mastered, the accomplished calligrapher possesses an ability few others can duplicate, so demands for the calligrapher's work can be high.

With the advent of desktop publishing, the special appeal of calligraphy faces a serious challenge. With the right computer software and a sophisticated printer, an otherwise untrained person can produce work that mimics hand lettering in a fraction of the time needed for traditional calligraphy. With a choice of type styles and the ability to correct mistakes almost instantly, any skilled computer user can produce material that rivals that of the accomplished calligrapher. Accordingly, some people think that calligraphy is doomed to become an obsolete field. Others disagree. They contend that the appeal of work done by hand may actually increase, serving as one counterpoint to an increasingly depersonalized, highly technological society. If this is true, then people will always be willing to pay a premium for the beautiful work that skilled calligraphers are able to produce.

For more information, contact:

Association for the Calligraphic Arts
2774 Countryside Boulevard, Number 2
Clearwater, FL 33761
www.calligraphicarts.org

Society of Scribes
PO Box 933
New York, NY 10150
www.societyofscribes.org

Washington Calligraphers Guild
PO Box 3688
Merrifield, VA 22116
www.calligraphersguild.org

Westcoast Calligraphy Society
Box 18150
2225 West Forty-First Avenue
Vancouver, BC V6M 4L3
Canada
www.galileo.spaceports.com/~callig

Greeting Card Illustrator

When was the last time you bought a greeting card? Were you impressed with the number and variety of cards available? The fact is, people purchase millions of greeting cards every year. Most greeting cards consist of verbal messages with drawings or other illustrations. These cards would not be possible without the work of greeting card illustrators.

Illustrators fill several types of roles in the greeting card industry. Some work exclusively as illustrators for large companies that specialize in greeting cards. Others work in smaller companies. Some work independently of any one company, either freelancing as illustrators or collaborating with writers to produce their own line of cards. Some individuals who are talented at both art and writing may combine the two functions, running their own small businesses that include producing and marketing cards.

Illustrators of greeting cards work in much the same way as do other illustrators. Most of their time is spent at drawing boards or computer consoles. Those who work as full-time employees of greeting card companies may have their own offices or designated work spaces. Illustrators who own their own businesses may rent office space or work out of their homes.

As with other types of illustrators, this work involves a collaborative process. Unless the illustrator is also a writer, the creative process involves responding to written work produced by a writer or concept specialist. Typically, the illustrator reads written copy and then comes up with one or more possible illustrations, usually in the form of rough sketches. Then an editor, writer, or other member of a work group reviews the drafts, possibly suggest changes, and make a selection. The illustrator then follows up by producing the finished illustration.

In some cases, illustrations may be discussed in advance so that a writer or editor can explain what is desired. In other instances, it is up to the illustrator to originate ideas. Occasionally, the process may be reversed, with the illustrator initiating an idea and a writer coming up with wording to match it.

What are the best features about a career in illustrating greeting cards? One is the variety involved. Some greeting cards are serious. Others are humorous. They may be directed at men, women, children, graduates, sick people, lovers, or any of dozens of other target groups. Illustrators may produce cartoon-like drawings, landscapes, or holiday scenes. To appeal to buyers, there is always a demand to come up with something new. As a result, the work offers a great deal of variety and a dominant spirit of creativity.

Another favorable point is the popularity of greeting cards. Unlike some types of craftspeople who may see limited demand for their work, illustrators of greeting cards help provide a product that is in great demand as a mainstream commodity. Only a small percentage of the population will ever buy a hand-woven rug, for instance. But check out the card section of the nearest Wal-Mart the day before Mother's Day, and you will see a good example of the universal appeal of greeting cards.

While there are no specific educational requirements for working in this field, most greeting card companies prefer people with a college or trade-school education in graphic design, art, or a related field. Experience in computer graphics may also be required. Freelancers or those who start their own businesses may set their own requirements. Certainly, they need polished skills in drawing, painting, and other related areas. To impress potential employers or clients, a portfolio of drawings or other work may be required.

Experienced illustrators who have specialized in greeting cards can easily make the transition to other related jobs should they desire. Their skills can be applied to positions as graphic artists, technical illustrators, or other occupations with similar demands.

For more information, contact:

Greeting Card Association
1156 Fifteenth Street NW, Suite 900
Washington, DC 20005
www.greetingcard.org

Cartoonist

One of the most individualistic of all careers is that of cartoonist. In a way, being a cartoonist is like being a novelist, essayist, or poet. The work is expressive, original, and creative. Usually it comes not as some externally mandated task, as is often the case for an illustrator, but rather from the imagination of the artist. For example, consider the work of famous cartoonists such as Gary Larson, the creator of the zany series *The Far Side*, or Charles Schultz, who became wealthy by creating Snoopy and all the Peanuts gang.

An overview of career possibilities for cartoonists contains both good news and bad news. The good news is that cartoonists can enjoy wonderful, stimulating careers. They do enjoyable work, which, if printed in newspapers or magazines, also can be enjoyed by thousands or even millions of people.

The bad news is that relatively few people actually succeed at making a full-time, paying occupation of drawing cartoons. Of course, some people do make this their profession, and there will always be room for more, so this is still a career worth considering for those who are both talented and persistent.

While the daily comic pages in newspapers might be the first thing that comes to mind when one considers the work of cartoonists, the field has many other possibilities. For example, political cartoons, found on most editorial pages, represent a specialty of their own. Many magazines also publish cartoons, most of which are designed to stand alone rather than be part of a series. Cartoonists are also employed by the motion picture industry and by publishers of comic books or graphic novels.

One way to get started in this field is to study art in a college or art school program and make cartooning a major emphasis of class projects and other efforts. The work produced then can become part of a portfolio to show to prospective employers.

Another approach is to pursue cartooning on a freelance basis. Here, the best way may be to start small by developing a regular cartoon feature for a school or neighborhood newspaper, then use that experience to approach a larger newspaper—or even better, regional or national syndicates. Individual cartoons also can be submitted to magazines that consider freelance submissions of cartoons. You can find more information about places to sell cartoons in the book *Humor and Cartoon Markets*, published annually by Writer's Digest Books (1507 Dana Avenue, Cincinnati, OH 45207; www.writersdigest.com).

For more information about careers in cartooning, contact the following organizations:

Graphic Artists Guild
90 John Street, Suite 403
New York, NY 10038
www.gag.org

National Cartoon Museum
PO Box 17M
Empire State Building 3304
New York, NY 10018
www.cartoon.org

Medical Illustrator

Take one part art and one part science, and the result is an important yet unusual craft: medical illustration.

If you have ever glanced through an encyclopedia or killed time in a doctor's examining room by studying wall posters with their drawings of various parts of the human body, you have seen firsthand the work of medical illustrators. Men and women who hold jobs in this field constitute a small but vital profession. They render detailed drawings of human anatomy for reproduction in books, slides, videotapes, and other media. These materials are used for science classes, medical school classes, and other instructional purposes.

The work of medical illustrators covers not just the way organs or other body parts look but also how they function. For example, an illustrator may draw a series of pictures of white blood cells to show how they attack and kill invading bacteria. Illustrators may also develop drawings and diagrams of medical processes. For instance, an illustrator might work closely with a surgeon who has developed a new surgical technique. The illustrator develops drawings that show, on a step-by-step basis, how the surgery is conducted. The finished drawings can then be used to help medical students or practicing surgeons learn the procedure.

The old adage "one picture is worth a thousand words" certainly holds true in this field. A carefully rendered medical illustration can hold tremendous value for those who must master complex concepts and techniques.

Because of its specialized nature, this field requires advanced training, typically a master's degree in medical illustration and a bachelor's degree in art or a scientific field, such as biology, anatomy, or zoology. Only a few schools offer such programs. Those accredited by the American Medical Association's Committee on Allied Health Education and Accreditation (CAHEA) include:

The Medical College of Georgia
1120 Fifteenth Street
Augusta, GA 30912
www.mcg.edu

The University of Illinois at Chicago
1919 West Taylor Street
Chicago, IL 60612
www.uic.edu

The Johns Hopkins School of Medicine
1830 East Monument Street, Suite 7000
Baltimore, MD 21205
www.med.jhu.edu/medart

The University of Texas Southwestern Medical Center
   at Dallas
5323 Harry Hines Boulevard
Dallas, TX 75235
www.utsouthwestern.edu

The University of Toronto
One King's College Circle
Toronto, ON M5S 1A8
Canada
www.utoronto.ca

The Association of Medical Illustrators provides publications and other membership services, which include some funding for scholarships, summer internship programs, and certification programs.
For more information, contact:

Association of Medical Illustrators
245 First Street, Suite 1800
Cambridge, MA 02142
www.ami.org

Book and Magazine Illustrator

If medical illustration seems too specialized for your interests, keep in mind that there is always a demand for general illustrators for books, magazines, and other publications. Any time you pick up a book or magazine, chances are you will see drawings, paintings, or other illustrations.

Some illustrators are employed as full-time staff members by book publishing companies or magazine publishers. Their usual role involves a three-step process:

1. reading written material developed by a writer or editor
2. coming up with a drawing or other illustration that enhances or illuminates a key concept
3. revising illustrations in response to suggestions by editors

Illustrators who are not employed on a full-time or permanent basis work as freelancers. In this case, the basic tasks performed are the same as for full-time staffers, but the illustrators work out of their own studios, typically in their homes. In addition, their relationships with editors differ. They may work for any number of magazines or publishing companies at any given time. Too, a good portion of their work may be spent on business details as opposed to the actual work of illustration. Typically, such tasks include contacting editors or art directors to drum up business, packing drawings and sending them by mail or delivery service, and keeping track of invoices, payments, and so forth.

In some cases, illustrators collaborate with writers to develop children's books or other projects before they are submitted to publishing companies. More often, however, their work is done after a manuscript has been written and scheduled for publication.

To succeed in this field, illustrators need the ability to produce clear, recognizable drawings, paintings, or graphic designs. They must work quickly enough to meet deadlines. Another helpful trait is the ability to read perceptively, since the crux of their work is enhancing the written word.

Training options vary. Most illustrators study commercial art or some other type of art in trade schools, art schools, community colleges, or four-year colleges and universities. Before landing jobs or freelance assignments, they usually develop portfolios that include representative samples of their work.

Cartographer

Cartographers design and produce maps. Their work combines the elements of science with the artistic work of drawing and illustrating. Some positions in this field emphasize the former, while others include the graphic skills needed for the production and printing of maps.

Most cartographers study geography at the college level. Some students focus on research or mapping sciences, such as the interpretation of satellite photos. Others, whose work is more likely to appeal to crafty people, specialize in typography or drawing. Most cartographers use both hand duplication and computer programs to produce maps and their components. As in other fields, the use of computers is becoming an increasingly important part of the overall work of those involved in cartography.

The American Congress on Surveying and Mapping is a major organization whose membership includes those interested in cartography. Among other services, this group provides a variety of publications related to cartography. For more information, contact:

American Congress on Surveying and Mapping
6 Montgomery Village Avenue, Suite 403
Gaithersburg, MD 20879
www.acsm.net

American Society for Photogrammetry and Remote Sensing
5410 Grosvenor Lane, Suite 210
Bethesda, MD 20814
www.asprs.org

North American Cartographic Information Society
PO Box 399
Milwaukee, WI 53201
www.nacis.org

Other Graphics Jobs

This chapter has provided an overview of several jobs of interest to crafty people. Some related jobs include the following:

- **Commercial artists** play a generalist's role. They use artistic skills to produce work requested by clients. They may produce anything from logos to newspaper ads. More and more, their work is done by computer rather than by hand. Commercial artists may also be known as graphic designers.
- **Desktop publishers** use computers to produce printed works. While some emphasize the writing aspect of this work, others concentrate on the amazing array of graphic images that can be produced with desktop publishing software.
- **Glass decorators** take glass objects and add their own decorations through painting or other techniques. A similar job is performed by pottery decorators.
- **Fashion artists** specialize in creating graphic designs of clothing and related items. They may create sketches of new designs based on descriptions provided by fashion designers or perhaps re-create existing pieces for use in catalogs or advertisements.
- **Painting restorers** take old or damaged paintings and painstakingly restore them as closely as possible to their original quality. Their work requires both artistic skill and the knowledge of special techniques for duplicating styles and materials used in earlier times.
- **Photograph retouchers** use artistic skills to improve the quality of photographs. They remove or cover blemishes and add attractive touches to make photos more appealing.
- **Printers** perform a variety of tasks related to the reproduction of written and graphic materials. In some cases, such as in small print shops, their work may include elements of graphic art and design.
- **Tattoo artists** are perhaps the only craftspeople who work on people rather than paper, canvas, or other media. With the health risks now identified with tattooing, some who work in this area are beginning to adopt methods more akin

to painting than traditional invasive techniques. At any rate, this stands as one occupation that is a far cry from the ordinary nine-to-five office job.

- **Tile decorators** add artistic images to ceramic tile and related materials. In some cases, this means using different colored tiles to produce an overall image.

Further Reading

Books

Browning, Marie. *Creative Craft Lettering Made Easy*. North Light Books, 2005.

Cicale, Annie. *The Art & Craft of Hand Lettering: Techniques, Projects, Inspiration*. Sterling Publishing Company, 2004.

Daubney, Margaret. *Calligraphy*. Crowood Press, 2004.

Elvin, Emmett. *Learn to Draw Cartoons: A Step-by-Step Guide*. Barnes & Noble Books, 2004.

Fishel, Catherine. *How to Grow as a Graphic Designer*. Allworth Press, 2004.

Fisher, Jeff. *The Savvy Designer's Guide to Success: Ideas and Tactics for a Killer Career*. F+W Publications, 2004.

Giarrano, Vincent. *Comics Crash Course*. F+W Publications, 2004.

Gordon, Barbara. *Opportunities in Commercial Art and Graphic Design Careers*. McGraw-Hill, 2003.

Hart, Christopher. *Cartoon Cool: How to Draw New Retro-Style Characters*. Watson-Guptill Publications, 2005.

Hartas, Leo. *How to Draw and Sell Digital Cartoons*. Barron's Educational Series, 2004.

Heller, Stephen, and Mirko Ilic. *Handwritten: Expressive Lettering in the Digital Age*. Thames and Hudson, 2004.

Linde, Riccard. *Game Art: Creation, Direction, and Careers*. Charles River Media, 2005.

Lovett, Patricia. *Teach Yourself Calligraphy*. McGraw-Hill, 2004.

Manley, Mike; Bret Blevin; Dave Gibbons; Jerry Ordway; and Genndy Tartakovsky. *The Best Of Draw! Volume 1.* TwoMorrows Publishing, 2004.

Marchant, Steve. *The Cartoonist's Workshop*. Collins & Brown, 2004.

Mehigan, Janet, and Mary Noble. *Beginner's Guide to Calligraphy: A Simple Three-Stage Guide to Perfect Letter Art.* Chartwell Books, 2005.

Newhall, Arthur, and Eugene Metcalf. *Learn the Art of Calligraphy: A Complete Kit for Beginners.* Barnes & Noble Books, 2004.

Patmore, Chris. *Character Design Studio: Create Cutting-Edge Cartoon Figures for Comic Books, Computer Games, and Graphic Novels.* Barnes & Noble Books, 2005.

Thomson, George. *Digital Calligraphy with Photoshop*. Course Technology, Inc., 2004.

Yue, Rebecca. *Chinese Calligraphy Made Easy: A Structured Course in Creating Beautiful Brush Lettering.* Watson-Guptill Publications, 2005.

Magazines

Applied Arts
18 Wynford Drive
Toronto, ON M3C 3S2
Canada
www.appliedartsmag.com

Cartographic Perspectives
North American Cartographic Information Society
PO Box 399
Milwaukee, WI 53201
www.nacis.org

Greetings etc.
4 Middlebury Boulevard
Randolph, NJ 07869
www.greetingsmagazine.com

HOW Magazine
F+W Publications
4700 East Galbraith Road
Cincinnati, OH 45236
www.howdesign.com

Letter Arts Review
212 Hillsboro Drive
Silver Spring, MD 20902
www.johnnealbooks.com

CHAPTER SEVEN

Odds and Ends

Some occupations do not fit readily into any of the craft categories explored in previous chapters. This chapter, therefore, offers a brief overview of several additional craft areas that may be of interest to crafty types.

Manager of a Craft-Related Enterprise

In many craft-related occupations, circumstances can lead to an area of endeavor that differs greatly from craft work itself: management. Becoming a manager may be a step you plan for, or it may be something that just happens. In either case, the prospect of becoming a manager is something every craftsperson should consider.

For example, say you start your own business as a cabinetmaker. Your initial intent is to operate as a one-person shop, and for the first couple of years this is the way that you proceed. But as business expands, the need for staff help becomes apparent. So you hire an assistant. Suddenly, you are a manager! This involves all kinds of details that will demand your time and attention. How much should you pay? What tasks should be assigned to the assistant? What hours should be worked? These are fairly simple questions, but they are merely the start of the decision-making process.

Once the employer-employee relationship is established, other questions will arise. How do you motivate the employee to do a good job? What happens if he or she frequently shows up late for work, seems to be sick all the time, or works too slowly? How do you handle a situation in which an employee's mistake ruins a job or in which a customer complains of being treated rudely by your assistant? We can't provide easy answers to these questions. The point is, unless you operate as a business composed of a single person, the need to manage people may surface. Even if you are employed by a small or large business, management opportunities may develop. Whether you supervise just one part-time worker or a staff of full-time craftspeople, you are a manager.

In any management situation, your skill as a craftsperson will be irrelevant. Instead of using your knowledge and manual dexterity to create interesting products, you will be using communication and organizational skills to supervise the work of others.

Should you ever find it necessary to take on management responsibilities in your career, following steps such as these will help you be successful:

- Take classes or seminars in topics such as supervisory skills, basic personnel management, employee motivation, or managing creative people.
- Enroll in a home-study course offered by the American Management Association.
- Read books and magazine articles about management.
- Observe other managers in action and learn from styles and techniques that you find effective.

Although managing people is important, you may also need to develop other types of business and management skills, such as business writing and maintaining financial records. The same strategies listed above can be effective in mastering skills in these areas. For more information, contact:

American Management Association
1601 Broadway
New York, NY 10019
www.amanet.org

Organ Builder

Organ builders practice a unique, highly specialized craft. Workers in this field build pipe or other types of organs, many of them quite large. Typically, the organs they build are used in churches.

Organ builders work with wood, metal, and other materials. Unlike many craft areas, the end result is a single unit that can take months and several people working together to produce.

Most organ builders learn the craft by participating in a formal apprenticeship program sponsored by the American Institute of Organbuilders and the U.S. Department of Labor. This program combines on-the-job training with courses of instruction such as the following:

- General Musical Background
- Introduction to Organ Building
- History of the Organ
- General Woodworking
- The Organ in its Environment
- Metalworking
- Technical Design and Execution
- Tonal Design
- Chest Building
- Pipe Making
- Wind Systems
- Business Administrative Management
- Organ Servicing
- Language Study (usually German)

It takes most people several years to complete an apprenticeship as an organ builder. Those with at least six thousand hours of experience who pass a proficiency exam achieve the status of journeyman. The more advanced status of master organ builder takes at least twelve thousand hours of experience along with other requirements.

Most organ builders work for companies that manufacture organs or other musical instruments. They may specialize in specific areas of organ building. Some focus on repairing rather than building organs, a job that often offers the chance to travel around the United States and Canada. To be successful, organ builders need patience, tenacity, and skill in working with different materials. A love and understanding of music is also helpful.

The American Institute of Organbuilders includes members from across North America. This group sponsors conventions, seminars, publications, and other opportunities for professional growth. For more information, contact:

American Institute of Organbuilders
PO Box 130982
Houston, TX 77219
www.pipeorgan.org

Associated Pipe Organ Builders of America
PO Box 155
Chicago Ridge, IL 60415
www.apoba.com

Taxidermist

Taxidermists prepare the bodies of fish, birds, mammals, and other animals for preservation and display. Their work requires not just an understanding of basic biology but also an artistic spirit. In performing their work, taxidermists exercise creativity as they try to make animals look both lifelike and interesting.

Some taxidermists work for museums. The overall purpose of their job is educational, with emphasis on preserving animals for public display. Their duties may include creating attractive displays of groups of animals as well as preserving individual specimens.

Other taxidermists operate their own businesses, working on a part-time or full-time basis. Primarily, they serve the needs of fishing enthusiasts and hunters who like to display their game as trophies. In addition to prize game fish, deer heads, and small game such as foxes or quail, they may deal with more exotic creatures, such as snakes or jungle animals.

Taxidermists generally learn their skills by taking classes or working with experienced professionals. Along with basic techniques of preservation and mounting, they may learn skills ranging from fur processing to creating realistic background displays.

Many working taxidermists belong to the National Taxidermists Association. This organization publishes an informative magazine and a newsletter providing information about matters such as legislation affecting the taxidermy industry. Association members receive a number of benefits, including educational seminars, conventions, and award programs.

For more information about careers in the field of taxidermy, contact:

Canadian Taxidermy Association
337 Bee Drive, RR 1
Millbrook, ON L0A 1G0
Canada

International Guild of Taxidermy
www.internationalguildoftaxidermy.org

National Taxidermists Association
108 Branch Drive
Slidell, LA 70461
www.nationaltaxidermists.com

. . . .

Teacher

"Those who can, do. Those who can't, teach." You have probably heard this old saying before, but don't believe it! This assertion is rarely true in any field, but it would be virtually impossible to succeed as a crafts teacher without some basic abilities in one or more craft areas. For those with such skills, teaching can provide a way for turning craft-related abilities into a paying job.

Teaching opportunities vary tremendously. They range from part-time or temporary positions teaching a single course or seminar to full-time positions teaching in schools or colleges. Teaching can be done on the side as a way to supplement income from direct work as a craftsperson. It can be a way for those with a job outside of craft areas to keep a hand in their fields of interest. Or it can provide a full-time career.

Teaching possibilities can be found in large cities, smaller towns, and rural areas. For the enterprising crafts practitioner, such opportunities can even be created. This might involve setting up seminars and offering them as an adjunct to a craft business. Or it might mean approaching a school and offering to teach courses that are not presently offered.

The continuing education divisions of community colleges, for example, are often receptive to suggestions for new classes. A letter or phone call proposing to teach noncredit classes or seminars in a specific craft area might well lead to teaching assignments.

For teaching jobs with craft schools, submission of a resume and portfolio may be required. A personal interview may also be needed. For temporary teaching jobs, another option is to present workshops for children in public schools. Check with principals or central office staff to explore such possibilities.

A totally different option is offered by summer camps, which often employ workshop leaders to teach crafts to children. This can be a real change of pace. After all, when was the last time you canoed in the lake at Camp Wichiwoomie? Even if you never attended a summer camp, you probably have a good idea of the typical setting: trees, a lake, counselors, and plenty of activities to entertain boys and girls for a week or more while their parents enjoy a strange and wonderful commodity—silence.

When parents need that break from the kids, somebody has to keep their offspring busy—and that someone could be you. Many summer camps employ instructors to teach a variety of crafts to children. Workshops in pottery, basket making, weaving, craft painting, and many other areas can be quite popular.

To locate jobs in summer camps, take steps such as these:

- Contact one of the following associations and ask for a listing of positions available as craft instructors:

  American Camp Association
  5000 State Road 67 North
  Martinsville, IN 46151
  www.acacamps.org

  Canadian Camping Association
  Box 74030
  Edmonton, AB T5K 2S7
  Canada
  www.ccamping.org

- Check for ads in magazines such as *American Craft*, in newspapers published in areas where camps are located, or on websites.
- Write to summer camps and ask if any positions are open for the period you have in mind. If you have had previous teaching experience of any kind (even if not related to crafts), be sure to mention it. Also discuss (or list in a resume) your craft competencies.
- Spread the word with friends, teachers, colleagues, or anyone else who might provide a job contact.

Working in a summer camp, as well as other types of teaching, can prove both challenging and beneficial. You can polish teaching skills while practicing your craft and earn some extra income in the process. Teaching may not be for everyone, but for those with an open mind, it can be fun!

Salesperson

Even if you never actually make anything, you can pursue a crafts-related career by selling the materials artisans need to make their products or by marketing completed craft products on behalf of practicing craftspeople. If you are primarily a craftsperson but need to enhance your income, selling supplies lets you supplement your craft sales and buy your own supplies at wholesale prices.

The market potential for crafts-related supplies is great. In addition to professionals, millions of hobbyists represent potential customers. Schools and colleges also purchase the supplies that students need in classes and seminars.

One career option in this area is working as a sales representative for a manufacturer. This might involve selling products on a wholesale basis to stores and shops or working directly with the public through telephone sales.

Another possibility is working for a retail store or crafts supplier. Here, you might serve as a clerk, sales associate, or manager. Customers might include professionals, hobbyists, or both.

Still another option is running your own craft supply business. This could be a home-based business or a full-fledged retail store.

In any case, selling to others requires good human relations skills as well as a talent for organization. For the energetic and motivated person, sales work can provide a rewarding alternative or supplement to a crafts career.

For more information on careers in crafts sales, contact the following organizations:

American Home Business Association
1981 Murray Holladay Road, Suite 225
Salt Lake City, UT 84117
www.homebusiness.com

Canadian Craft and Hobby Association
Number 24, 1410 Fortieth Avenue NE
Calgary, AB T2E 6L1
Canada
www.cdncraft.org

Craft and Hobby Association
319 East Fifty-Fourth Street
Elmwood Park, NJ 07407
www.hobby.org

U.S. Small Business Administration
409 Third Street SW
Washington, DC 20416
www.sba.gov

Watermark Association of Artisans
150 Highway 158 East
Camden, NC 27921
www.albemarle-nc.com/camden/watermark

Further Reading

Books

Audsley, George Ashdown. *The Organ of the Twentieth Century*. Dover Publications, 2004.

Edwards, Paul; Peter Economy; and Sarah Edwards. *Home-Based Business for Dummies*. John Wiley & Sons, 2005.

Lownes-Jackson, Millicent, and Leah Grubbs. *Starting a Craft Business: The Indispensable Guide to Starting a Business for the Creative Artisan*. Business of Your Own, 2005.

Moyer, John W. *Practical Taxidermy*. Krieger Publishing Company, 2000.

Rosen, Wendy, and Anne Childress. *Crafting as a Business*. Sterling Publishing Company, 1998.

Thistlethwaite, Nicholas; John Butt; and Laurence Dreyfus. *Making of the Victorian Organ*. Cambridge University Press, 1999.

Triplet, Todd. *The Complete Guide to Small Game Taxidermy: How to Work with Squirrels, Varmints, and Predators*. The Lyons Press, 2003.

Triplett, Todd. *The Complete Guide to Turkey Taxidermy: How to Prepare Fans, Boards, and Full-Body Mounts*. Lyons Press, 2003.

Weltman, Barbara; Shirley Muse; and Kara Gordon *The Complete Idiot's Guide to Starting an e-Bay Business*. Alpha Books, 2005.

Magazines

The Crafts Report
100 Rogers Road
Wilmington, DE 19801
www.craftsreport.com

Crafts 'n Things
Clapper Communications Companies
2400 Devon, Suite 375
Des Plaines, IL 60018
www.craftideas.com

CHAPTER EIGHT

Breaking In

In our complex world, there are literally thousands of different occupations. Within each job category, however, the number of people actually holding down a paying job may vary tremendously. Certainly, you can't pick up the Sunday newspaper or access a website and find thirty classified ads for wood-carvers or stained glass makers. On the other hand, people do hold jobs carving wood, making stained glass, and pursuing many other craft areas. The question is not whether a crafts career is possible, but how one can get started.

Pursuing a crafts career is similar to going after other types of jobs in some ways but quite different in others. Here is a brief overview of strategies to follow in getting started. Any one person probably will not need to follow all of these steps but will want to try at least some of them.

Visit Arts and Crafts Fairs

Arts and crafts fairs are common events held frequently around the country, especially during the spring and summer. To get a firsthand look at various crafts, visit such fairs. Stroll around and check out different crafts. Talk to craftspeople about their work. Pay attention to the crowd and see which types of crafts seem most popular with the general public. If you have not yet focused on a particular craft area, use this process to help identify those that seem a good match with your own interests. If you have identified a craft specialty, seek out others in the same area and compare notes.

Read About Crafts

Because crafts are so popular, a great deal of written material is available about them. Most of the chapters in this book include listings of craft magazines and books on specific crafts. Use these lists as a starting point in your reading. Visit a local bookstore and pick up a few books. If preferred titles are not available, most stores will order them for you at no extra charge.

A less costly option is consulting a local library. Even small libraries may subscribe to magazines such as *American Craft*, which covers a wide range of craft areas. Most libraries should also have books about craft topics and can obtain others through interlibrary loan programs.

Take Craft Classes

As noted throughout this book, classes in different craft areas are common. Enrolling in a class takes you a step further than reading or visiting craft fairs, for being a student provides actual hands-on experience. This not only teaches you fundamental skills but also helps you determine whether a given craft area is right for you. It's one thing to read about making pottery, for instance, but quite another to do it.

Craft classes vary immensely in scope, setting, and price. Some classes presented as summer seminars, for example, are rather expensive. Others, such as those offered through community colleges, can be quite reasonable.

Unless you are interested in a full-fledged degree or diploma program, you need not worry about tests, final grades, or similar concerns. Most craft classes are offered on a noncredit basis without exams or grading.

Some of the sponsors of craft classes include:

- arts and crafts schools
- community, junior, and technical colleges

- trade schools or "career colleges"
- extension or continuing education divisions of four-year colleges and universities
- public school districts with adult and community education programs
- county or city recreation departments
- churches, YMCAs, or other community organizations
- practicing craftspeople who offer their own lessons or classes

To find out about classes or workshops, contact schools and ask for a catalog or schedule of classes. Most schools are glad to provide publications and will furnish all the information you need.

Experiment with Different Crafts

Unless you have already committed to a single craft area, try out several crafts before settling on a given specialty. This might consist of taking classes or simply obtaining the necessary materials and completing a basic project or two. The approach here may be closer to that of the craft hobbyist than the craft professional, but a little diversity never hurts. Who knows? You might discover a flair for a craft you never previously considered. Conversely, you might find that a craft that seemed appealing is not that enjoyable to you after all and save yourself a considerable investment of time and money.

Learn from the Experts

In the Middle Ages and much more recently, the only way to learn a craft was to serve as an apprentice to an accomplished craftsperson. This was a long, involved, and highly structured process, but it paid off. Today, formal apprenticeships are less common, but you can utilize a variation of the process to break into the craft area of your choice.

At its most basic level, this might consist simply of visiting practicing craftspeople and asking questions about their work. Ask about special techniques, sources of raw materials, how their work is selling, problems they have encountered, where they buy equipment, and so forth.

For a more intensive experience, offer to serve as a part-time assistant. Be willing to work on an unpaid basis if necessary, with the chance to learn about the craft in lieu of payment. If the craftsperson is highly successful, a paying job might be a possibility. In either case, the main objective is to learn as much about the business as possible.

Develop Credentials

If you are selling work at arts and crafts fairs, the work will generally stand on its own. Your own background may not be relevant. In some cases, though, you may need to market not only your work but also yourself. For example, a potential customer may want to commission you to take on a project, or a school might consider you to teach a class. In these and other instances, having related credentials will be important.

There are many ways to develop credentials. In addition to work experience, here are some possibilities:

- complete a degree or diploma program
- complete an apprenticeship
- participate in seminars or short courses
- become certified by a craft organization
- compete in contests and win awards
- present talks, workshops, or seminars

Any of these steps can show others that you have special skills or knowledge—the real purpose of credentials.

Once you earn credentials, don't be shy about sharing them. Letting others know about your special credentials is not bragging, just good business. If you earn certificates or diplomas, display them. List credentials in resumes, brochures about you and your work, bio sheets, or other outlets. The more such information is distributed, the more successful you appear to others.

Also, consider developing a portfolio of your work. Samples (or photos of samples) of your work can serve as visual confirmation of your special skills.

Join Professional Organizations

One of the best ways to expand your horizons as a craftsperson is to join one or more professional organizations. Groups such as these can be helpful in getting your career started as well as in keeping it going. Through networking, sharing information, and a variety of other services, these groups provide important help to craftspeople.

If you join a professional organization, be an active participant. Stay in touch with other members and attend conventions, seminars, or other meetings if possible.

Previous chapters have listed various groups related to specific craft areas. A more general group is the American Craft Council. This national group fosters interests in crafts and provides a wide range of services to members. For more information, contact:

American Craft Council
72 Spring Street, Sixth Floor
New York, NY 10012
www.craftcouncil.org

Use the Internet

An area of great potential for developing a crafts career is the Internet. As each year passes, more and more people surf the World Wide Web, use e-mail, and otherwise take advantage of online communications.

No matter where you live, the Internet can link you to potential customers, other craftspeople, craft organizations, and other groups. Here are just some of the ways you can use the Internet to develop your crafts career:

- Create a Web page featuring you and your work.
- Use e-mail to communicate with customers or other craftspeople.
- Check out websites of other craftspeople to compare notes and seek out ideas.
- Develop e-commerce skills as a way to promote your craft business and sell crafts or craft-related products.

Just think. You can live in a New York town house, a Montreal apartment, or a log cabin in the Alaska wilderness. If you own a computer, you can link yourself to the rest of the world. In the process, you can pursue your craft-related interests without being isolated from kindred souls.

Take the First Step

Whatever strategies you choose in pursuing a crafts career, the most important move is taking the first step. (Actually, you could consider reading this book the first step; in that case, it's your next step that really counts!) If working in a craft area seems appealing, move from the mode of thinking about it to doing it.

Too risky? Then minimize the risk. Start small. Be a part-time craftsperson. Invest a little time and perhaps a small amount of money. Then if you enjoy the experience, expand the scope of your activities.

The Future for Crafty People

When one looks ahead, the future looks bright for people working in the various craft areas. This is not just empty optimism but a prediction based on factors such as these:

- The continued advance of technology will make hand-crafted products seem even more special.
- Nostalgia for the past will help keep many craft areas popular.
- While recessions may come and go, the number of people with discretionary income will continue to be large. There will be many people who are not only interested in craft products but able to afford them. This should be particularly true of the baby boom generation as it ages.
- The increasing level of international trade and travel should be a boon to craft producers and sellers. American arts and crafts are already popular in many nations, and this popularity should increase as more foreign tourists travel to North America and as trade between nations grows.

Crafts do have a bright future. The only question remaining is this: will you be a part of that future? Here's hoping the answer is a firm and optimistic yes.

Arts Agencies in the United States and Canada

The following agencies provide information on education and training as well as opportunities for practicing your craft in the various regions the organizations represent.

United States

Alabama State Council on the Arts
201 Monroe Street
Montgomery, AL 36130
www.arts.state.al.us

Alaska State Council on the Arts
411 West Fourth Avenue, Suite 1E
Anchorage, AK 99501
www.eed.state.ak.us/aksca

Arizona Commission on the Arts
417 West Roosevelt
Phoenix, AZ 85003
www.arizonaarts.org

Arkansas Arts Council
1500 Tower Building
323 Center Street
Little Rock, AR 72201
www.arkansasarts.com

California Arts Council
1300 I Street, Suite 930
Sacramento, CA 95814
www.cac.ca.gov

Colorado Council on the Arts
1380 Lawrence Street, Suite 1200
Denver, CO 80204
www.coloarts.state.co.us

Connecticut Commission on Culture and Tourism
Arts Division
One Financial Plaza
755 Main Street
Hartford, CT 06103
www.cultureandtourism.org/arts

Delaware Division of the Arts
Carvel State Office Building
820 North French Street
Wilmington, DE 19801
www.artsdel.org

Florida Arts
Division of Cultural Affairs
1001 DeSoto Park Drive
Tallahassee, FL 32301
www.florida-arts.org

Georgia Council for the Arts
260 Fourteenth Street NW, Suite 401
Atlanta, GA 30318
www.web-dept.com/gca

Hawaii State Foundation on Culture and the Arts
250 South Hotel Street, Second Floor
Honolulu, HI 96813
www.state.hi.us/sfca

Idaho Commission on the Arts
PO Box 83720
Boise, ID 83720
www.arts.idaho.gov

Illinois Arts Council
James R. Thompson Center
100 West Randolph Street, Suite 10-500
Chicago, IL 60601
www.state.il.us/agency/iac

Indiana Arts Commission
150 West Market Street, Suite 618
Indianapolis, IN 46204
www.in.gov/arts

Iowa Arts Council
Iowa Department of Cultural Affairs
600 East Locust
Des Moines, IA 50319
www.iowaartscouncil.org

Kansas Arts Council
700 Southwest Jackson, Suite 1004
Topeka, KS 66603
http://arts.state.ks.us

Kentucky Arts Council
Capital Plaza Tower, Twenty-First Floor
500 Mero Street
Frankfort, KY 40601
www.kyarts.org

Louisiana Division of the Arts
PO Box 44247
Baton Rouge, LA 70804
www.crt.state.la.us/arts

Maine Arts Commission
193 State Street
Augusta, ME 04333
www.mainearts.com

Maryland State Arts Council
175 West Ostend Street, Suite E
Baltimore, MD 21230
www.msac.org

Massachusetts Cultural Council
10 St. James Avenue, Third Floor
Boston, MA 02116
www.massculturalcouncil.org

Michigan Council for Arts and Cultural Affairs
History, Arts, and Libraries Department
702 West Kalamazoo
PO Box 30705
Lansing, MI 48909
www.michigan.gov

Minnesota State Arts Board
Park Square Court, Suite 200
400 Sibley Street
St. Paul, MN 55101
www.arts.state.mn.us

Mississippi Arts Commision
Woolfolk Building
501 North West Street, Suite 701B
Jackson, MS 39201
www.arts.state.ms.us

Missouri Arts Council
Wainwright State Office Complex
111 North Seventh Street, Suite 105
St. Louis, MO 63101
www.missouriartscouncil.org

Montana Arts Council
City County Building
316 North Park Avenue, Suite 252
PO Box 202201
Helena, MT 59620
www.art.state.mt.us

National Assembly of State Arts Agencies
1029 Vermont Avenue NW, Second Floor
Washington, DC 20005
www.nasaa-arts.org

Nebraska Arts Council
1004 Farnam Street, Plaza Level
Omaha, NE 68102
www.nebraskaartscouncil.org

Nevada Arts Council
716 North Carson Street, Suite A
Carson City, NV 89701
http://dmla.clan.lib.nv.us/docs/arts

New Hampshire State Council on the Arts
2 1/2 Beacon Street, Second Floor
Concord, NH 03301
www.state.nh.us/nharts

New Jersey State Council on the Arts
225 West State Street
PO Box 306
Trenton, NJ 08625
www.njartscouncil.org

New Mexico Arts
PO Box 1450
Santa Fe, NM 87504
www.nmarts.org

New York State Council on the Arts
175 Varick Street
New York, NY 10014
www.nysca.org

North Carolina Arts Council
Department of Cultural Resources
Jenkins House
221 East Lane Street
Raleigh, NC 27699
www.ncarts.org

North Dakota Council on the Arts
1600 East Century Avenue, Suite 6
Bismarck, ND 58503
www.state.nd.us/arts

Ohio Arts Council
727 East Main Street
Columbus, OH 43205
www.oac.state.oh.us

Oklahoma Arts Council
Jim Thorpe Building
PO Box 52001-2001
Oklahoma City, OK 73152
www.oklaosf.state.ok.us/~arts

Oregon Arts Commission
775 Summer Street NE, Suite 200
Salem, OR 97301
www.oregonartscommission.org

Pennsylvania Council on the Arts
216 Finance Building
Harrisburg, PA 17120
www.pacouncilonthearts.org

Rhode Island State Council on the Arts
One Capitol Hill, Third Floor
Providence, RI 02908
www.arts.ri.gov

South Carolina Arts Commission
1800 Gervais Street
Columbia, SC 29201
www.state.sc.us/arts

South Dakota Arts Council
South Dakota State Library Building
800 Governors Drive
Pierre, SD 57501
www.artscouncil.sd.gov

Tennessee Arts Commission
Citizens Plaza
401 Charlotte Avenue
Nashville, TN 37243
www.arts.state.tn.us

Texas Commission on the Arts
PO Box 13406
Austin, TX 78711
www.arts.state.tx.us

Utah Arts Council
617 East South Temple
Salt Lake City, UT 84102
http://arts.utah.gov

Vermont Arts Council
136 State Street, Drawer 33
Montpelier, VT 05633
www.vermontartscouncil.org

Virginia Commission for the Arts
223 Governor Street, Second Floor
Richmond, VA 23219
www.arts.virginia.gov

Washington State Arts Commission
711 Capital Way South, Suite 600
PO Box 42675
Olympia, WA 98504
www.arts.wa.gov

West Virginia Commission on the Arts
1900 Kanawha Boulevard East
Charleston, WV 25305
www.wvculture.org/arts

Wisconsin Arts Board
101 East Wilson Street, First Floor
Madison, WI 53702
www.arts.state.wi.us

Wyoming Arts Council
2320 Capitol Avenue
Cheyenne, WY 82002
http://wyoarts.state.wy.us

Canada

Canada Council for the Arts
350 Albert Street
PO Box 1047
Ottawa, ON K1P 5V8
Canada
www.canadacouncil.ca

Community and Citizenship Services
Arts Development Branch
901 Standard Life Centre
10405 Jasper Avenue
Edmonton, AB T5J 4R7
Canada
www.cd.gov.ab.ca

Manitoba Arts Council
525 - 93 Lombard Avenue
Winnipeg, MB R3B 3B1
Canada
www.artscouncil.mb.ca

New Brunswick Arts Council
39 King Street
Saint John, NB E2L 4W3
Canada
www.nbac.ca

Newfoundland and Labrador Arts Council
PO Box 98
St. John's, NL A1C 5H5
Canada
www.nlac.nf.ca

Nova Scotia Department of Tourism and Culture
Culture Division
1800 Argyle Street, Suite 402
Halifax, NS B3J 2R5
Canada
www.gov.ns.ca/dtc/culture

Nunavut Arts and Crafts Association
PO Box 1539
Iqaluit, NU X0A 0H0
Canada
www.nacaarts.org

Ontario Arts Council
151 Bloor Street West, Fifth floor
Toronto, ON M5S 1T6
Canada
www.arts.on.ca

Organization of Saskatchewan Arts Councils
1102 Eighth Avenue
Regina, SK S4R 1C9
Canada
www.osac.sk.ca

Québec—Conseil des arts et des lettres du Québec
79 Boulevard René-Lévesque Est, Troisième Étage
Québec, QC G1R 5N5
Canada
www.calq.gouv.qc.ca

About the Author

Mark Rowh is a writer and educator based in Dublin, Virginia. His experience has included administrative positions at colleges in Virginia, West Virginia, and South Carolina.

Rowh is a widely published writer. His articles on education, business, management, and general-interest topics have appeared in more than eighty national magazines. He is the author of a number of other books, including the McGraw-Hill publications *Careers in Real Estate* and *Great Jobs for Political Science Majors*.